GAS GIANTS

How to use this book

Welcome to *Space Science*. All the books in this set are organized to help you through the multitude of pictures and facts that make this subject so interesting. There is also a master glossary for the set on pages 58–64 and an index on pages 65–72.

The text is organized into chapters.

Photographs and diagrams have been carefully selected and annotated for clarity. Captions provide more facts.

Capitals show key glossary terms. They are defined in the quick reference glossary.

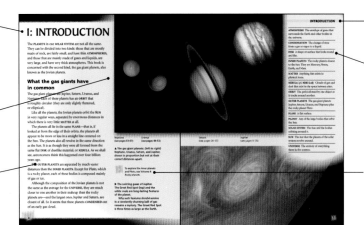

Chapter heading.

Quick reference glossary. All these glossary entries, sometimes with further explanation, appear in the master glossary for the set on pages 58–64.

Links to related information in other titles in the *Space Science* set.

 Atlantic Europe Publishing

First published in 2004 by
Atlantic Europe Publishing Company Ltd.

Copyright © 2004
Atlantic Europe Publishing Company Ltd.

Author
Brian Knapp, BSc, PhD

Art Director
Duncan McCrae, BSc

Senior Designer
Adele Humphries, BA, PGCE

Editors
Mary Sanders, BSc, and Gillian Gatehouse

Illustrations on behalf of Earthscape Editions
David Woodroffe and David Hardy

Design and production
EARTHSCAPE EDITIONS

Print
WKT Company Limited, Hong Kong

This product is manufactured from sustainable managed forests. For every tree cut down, at least one more is planted.

Space science – **Volume 5: Gas giants**
A CIP record for this book is available from the British Library

ISBN 1 86214 367 6

All photographs and diagrams NASA except the following:
(c=center t=top b=bottom l=left r=right)

Earthscape Editions 17, 29br, 37b, 40–41b, 44–45b, 50cr, 55t; *NASA Artists* 9t, 11, 24b, 26, 27, 29tr, 32tl, 34bl, 35, *D. Seal* 6–7b, 37t, *and Ken Hodges* 12–13.

The front cover features the planet Saturn; the back cover, (*from left to right*) Neptune, Uranus, and Jupiter.

NASA, the U.S. National Aeronautics and Space Administration, was founded in 1958 for aeronautical and space exploration. It operates several installations around the country and has its headquarters in Washington, D.C.

CONTENTS

▶ The great turbulence in Neptune's atmosphere produces storms or upwelling gases that can be seen as dark spots.

1: INTRODUCTION

The **PLANETS** in our **SOLAR SYSTEM** are not all the same. They can be divided into two kinds: those that are mostly made of rock, are fairly small, and have thin **ATMOSPHERES**, and those that are mainly made of gases and liquids, are very large, and have very thick atmospheres. This book is concerned with the second kind, the gas giant planets, also known as the Jovian planets.

What the gas giants have in common

The gas giant planets are Jupiter, Saturn, Uranus, and Neptune. Each of these planets has an **ORBIT** that is roughly circular (they are only slightly flattened, or elliptical).

Like all the planets, the Jovian planets orbit the **SUN** in very regular ways, separated by enormous distances in which there is very little **MATTER** at all.

The planets all lie in the same **PLANE**—that is, if looked at from the edge of their orbits, the planets all appear to be more or less in a straight line centered on the Sun. The planets also all revolve in the same direction as the Sun. It is as though they were all formed from the same flat **DISK** of dustlike material, or **NEBULA**. As we shall see, astronomers think this happened over four billion years ago.

The **OUTER PLANETS** are separated by much vaster distances than the **INNER PLANETS**. Except for Pluto, which is a rocky planet, each of these bodies is composed mainly of gas or ice.

Although the composition of the Jovian planets is not the same as the average for the **UNIVERSE**, they are much closer to one another in their makeup than the rocky planets are—and the largest ones, Jupiter and Saturn, are closest of all. So it seems that these planets **CONDENSED** out of an early gas cloud.

Neptune
(see pages 52–57)

Uranus
(see pages 48–51)

▲ The gas giant planets: *(left to right)* Neptune, Uranus, Saturn, and Jupiter, shown in proportion but not at their correct distances apart.

To explore the inner planets and Pluto, see Volume 4: *Rocky planets*.

▶ The swirling gases of Jupiter. The Great Red Spot (top) and the white ovals are long-lasting features of the planet.
   Why such features should survive in a constantly churning ball of gas remains a mystery. The Great Red Spot is three times as large as the Earth.

Saturn
(see pages 36–47)

Jupiter
(see pages 8–35)

ATMOSPHERE The envelope of gases that surrounds the Earth and other bodies in the universe.

CONDENSATION The change of state from a gas or vapor to a liquid.

DISK A shape or surface that looks round and flat.

INNER PLANETS The rocky planets closest to the Sun. They are Mercury, Venus, Earth, and Mars.

MATTER Anything that exists in physical form.

NEBULA (pl. **NEBULAE**) Clouds of gas and dust that exist in the space between stars.

ORBIT The path followed by one object as it tracks around another.

OUTER PLANETS The gas giant planets Jupiter, Saturn, Uranus, and Neptune plus the rocky planet Pluto.

PLANE A flat surface.

PLANET Any of the large bodies that orbit the Sun.

SOLAR SYSTEM The Sun and the bodies orbiting around it.

SUN The star that the planets of the solar system revolve around.

UNIVERSE The entirety of everything there is; the cosmos.

For **CONDENSATION** to have been an important process, we have to imagine that the giant planets formed as **SPACE** gradually became colder. As a result, some **ELEMENTS** stopped drifting around as gases and became first liquids and then solids.

In regions very distant from the warming **RADIATION** of the Sun space has become cold enough even for elements with low **BOILING POINTS**, such as ammonia and methane, to become liquids. That is the difference that separates the gas planets from the rocky planets. On the rocky planets ammonia and methane are present only as gases and readily escape from their atmospheres.

There is a big difference in size between the largest pair of gas giants—Jupiter and Saturn—and the smallest pair—Uranus and Neptune. This also points to some differences in composition and properties.

Uranus and Neptune are the smaller of the gas giants. They have **CORES** of rocky materials and contain simple metallic **COMPOUNDS**. But in addition, they have solid water, ammonia, and methane enveloping their rocky cores. They also have methane, helium, and hydrogen in their atmospheres. The biggest of the giants—Jupiter and Saturn—have hydrogen and helium in their cores. That makes them unique, since it takes an immensely powerful **GRAVITY** to compress these light gases into liquids.

Rings and moons

All the Jovian planets have rings that contain a mixture of ice and dust, and they have many **SATELLITES**: small captive bodies we more commonly call moons. These moons move around their planets just as the planets move around the Sun. Each moon behaves as though it were a planet, while the dust behaves as though it were an **ASTEROID BELT**.

▲ The solar system's largest moon, Ganymede (see pages 30–32), orbiting the gaseous world of Jupiter.

Ganymede, which, in contrast to Jupiter, is a rocky body, is larger than the planets Mercury and Pluto and Saturn's largest moon, Titan.

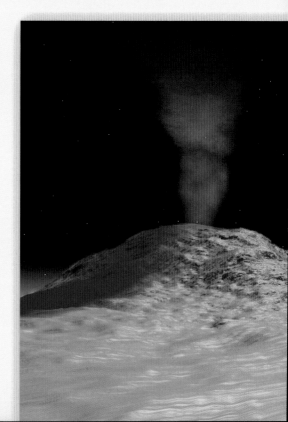

The giant planets have two types of moons orbiting them. There are those that follow a more or less circular orbit in the same plane as the planet's **EQUATOR** and revolve in the same direction as their parent planet. They are called the regular satellites. They were probably formed from gas and dust at the same time as the planet. But there are others that do not fit into the general pattern. Most of these moons are small and orbit far away from their parent. They have different orbits and often rotate in the opposite direction from their parents. They are known as irregular satellites. They are probably small bodies that were captured by the planets after they had formed elsewhere in the solar system.

The moons are enveloped in thin, flat rings. The rings themselves are made of countless billions of tiny rocky bodies. They might be the debris left over after the planet and larger moons formed. Alternatively, they might be debris left over after collisions of **METEOROIDS** with a former moon or moons. In the former case the rings would be as old as the planets, but in the latter case the rings would be younger. At the moment, we simply have no measurements to tell us which of these alternatives is true.

ASTEROID BELT The collection of asteroids that orbit the Sun between the orbits of Mars and Jupiter.

BOILING POINT The change of state of a substance in which a liquid rapidly turns into a gas without a change in temperature.

COMPOUND A substance made from two or more elements that have chemically combined.

CONDENSATION The change of state from a gas or vapor to a liquid.

CORE The central region of a body.

ELEMENT A substance that cannot be decomposed into simpler substances by chemical means.

EQUATOR The ring drawn around a body midway between the poles.

GRAVITY The force of attraction between bodies.

METEOROID A small body moving in the solar system that becomes a meteor if it enters the Earth's atmosphere.

RADIATION The transfer of energy in the form of waves (such as light and heat) or particles (such as from radioactive decay of a material).

SATELLITE An object that is in an orbit around another object, usually a planet.

SPACE Everything beyond the Earth's atmosphere.

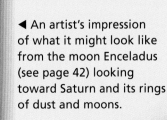

◀ An artist's impression of what it might look like from the moon Enceladus (see page 42) looking toward Saturn and its rings of dust and moons.

2: JUPITER

Jupiter is the real giant of the solar system. It is 318 times more massive than the Earth, with a volume 1,500 times as great.

It has an intense **MAGNETIC FIELD** and an internal heat source. It sends out to space more heat than it receives from the Sun. In **RADIO WAVES** Jupiter actually can send out more energy than the Sun.

Jupiter is almost big enough to have become a **STAR** in its own right. It is the fifth planet in distance from the Sun. It is visible with the naked eye and is named after the Roman ruler of the gods.

Although not as famed as Saturn for its rings, Jupiter has them, along with **MOONS** included in them, which are among the most spectacular of the bodies in the solar system. Jupiter's narrow rings include 16 moons, of which four are larger than our Moon and one bigger than the planet Mercury. The major moons (outward from the planet) are Io, Callisto, Ganymede, and Europa (see pages 21–34).

Much of our knowledge of Jupiter comes from the space **PROBES PIONEER** 10 and 11 and **VOYAGER** 1 and 2 (see page 27), all of which passed Jupiter in the late 1970s. We got so much information that it is still being analyzed.

▼ Jupiter—the giant of the solar system.

A lightweight, surfaceless planet

Despite its massive size and large **GRAVITY**, Jupiter is a lightweight planet, having a **DENSITY** of 1.3 g/cm³, only a bit more dense than water. It is less than a quarter as dense as the Earth. This, above all, tells us that the structure of Jupiter must be very different from that of the Earth.

Galileo

▶ Launched in October 1989, GALILEO entered orbit around Jupiter on December 7, 1995. The spacecraft's mission was to conduct detailed studies of the giant planet, its largest moons, and the Jovian magnetic environment.

The blue dots on the picture represent the data being sent up to Galileo by the atmospheric probe that was released to descend through the clouds (see page 12).

For more on Pioneer, Voyager, and Galileo see "Outer worlds" in Volume 6: *Journey into space*.

Jupiter does not have a land surface as we do on Earth. Instead, the gases in the CORE gradually become denser with depth, turning first into a liquid and then probably a solid as the core is approached. Jupiter appears to spin incredibly fast on its AXIS. But what we actually see are the gases of the ATMOSPHERE on the move. We have no means of telling whether or not the solid body at the center of the planet is spinning with the same speed.

ATMOSPHERE The envelope of gases that surrounds the Earth and other bodies in the universe.

AXIS (pl. **AXES**) The line around which a body spins.

CORE The central region of a body.

DENSITY A measure of the amount of matter in a space.

GALILEO A U.S. space probe launched in October 1989 and designed for intensive investigation of Jupiter.

GRAVITY The force of attraction between bodies.

MAGNETIC FIELD The region of influence of a magnetic body.

MOON The name generally given to any large natural satellite of a planet.

PIONEER A name for a series of unmanned U.S. spacecraft. Pioneer 1 was launched into lunar orbit on October 11, 1958. The others all went into deep space.

PROBE An unmanned spacecraft designed to explore our solar system and beyond.

RADIO WAVES A form of electromagnetic radiation, like light and heat.

STAR A large ball of gases that radiates light. The star nearest the Earth is the Sun.

VOYAGER A pair of U.S. space probes designed to provide detailed information about the outer regions of the solar system.

Features of the atmosphere

What we see of Jupiter is the atmosphere. It consists of light and dark bands—called belts—of gases that churn around the planet in opposite directions, much like gear wheels in a machine. Set among them are some relatively permanent features, of which the most well known and the largest is the **GREAT RED SPOT** (see page 14).

When we look at the surface atmosphere of Jupiter, we tend to see it in the same way as the atmosphere on Earth. On Earth we know that the churning pattern is produced by a swirling mass of gases called **CYCLONES** and **ANTICYCLONES** (commonly called highs and lows). Similar types of circular, or often slanted oval, features can be seen in the belts. This suggests that there are tremendous up-and-down flows of gases in the atmosphere.

▶ An artist's rendering of what it might look like to be within the clouds of Jupiter. The location of this view is similar to the site where the probe from the Galileo spacecraft entered Jupiter's atmosphere in 1995 (see page 12). The picture has a vertical exaggeration of 25 times.

▼ The atmosphere on Jupiter is unbelievably turbulent and often resembles gear wheels rotating in opposite directions. In addition, there are wavelike shapes. Such shapes often appear in rapidly moving fluids and are called standing waves.

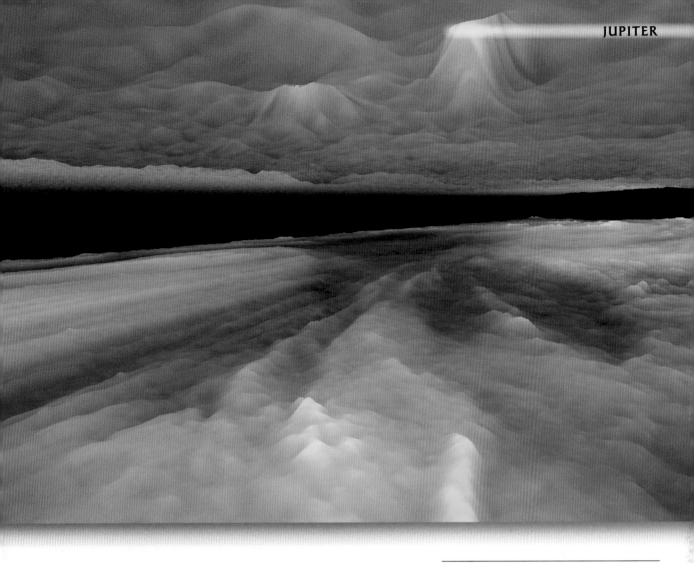

On Earth a pattern of highs and lows is caused by some gases spiraling up, while in other places gases are spiraling down (like water flowing out of a bath drain). But on Jupiter these eddies are immense—many bigger than our Earth! They are also colored, often with light pinks, yellows, and white, the significance of which is unclear.

On Earth the highs and lows often move from the tropics toward the **POLES** and vice versa. That is because they are moving between regions of cold and warmth. In particular, they are often associated with regions of land and ocean. On Jupiter they appear to be trapped at definite **LATITUDES**. That may be because Jupiter has no big temperature contrasts like the Earth and has no land or ocean, just a deep mass of gas.

ANTICYCLONE A roughly circular region of the atmosphere that is spiraling outward and downward.

CYCLONE A large storm in which the atmosphere spirals inward and upward.

GREAT RED SPOT A large, almost permanent feature of the Jovian atmosphere that moves around the planet at about latitude 23°S.

LATITUDE Angular distance north or south of the equator, measured through 90°.

POLE The geographic pole is the place where a line drawn along the axis of rotation exits from a body's surface.

▶ An artist's impression of what the upper Jovian atmosphere might have looked like as the small surface probe floated down from **GALILEO** to investigate the atmosphere. The probe has its **HEAT SHIELD** below and a parachute above.

The wok-shaped probe sent information to the orbiter for 57.6 minutes as it dropped about 200 kilometers through the atmosphere before succumbing to **ATMOSPHERIC PRESSURE** about 23 times greater than the average at Earth's sea level.

Jupiter's core is also the source of its heat. The heat may spread out evenly in all directions, warming the atmosphere from below and causing **CONVECTION CURRENTS** in the atmosphere. This source of convection is very different than on Earth, where little heat escapes from the core, and most heat in the atmosphere is soaked up by the land and oceans after **RADIATION** from the Sun. More heat is absorbed at the equator than at the poles, which causes air to flow between the equator and poles. On Jupiter, without any Sun heating thanks to its remoteness and with no temperature contrast between the poles and the equator, there may be no force to drive the eddies from one latitude to the other as there is on Earth. Rather, the contrasts might be most intense between the lower and upper atmospheres.

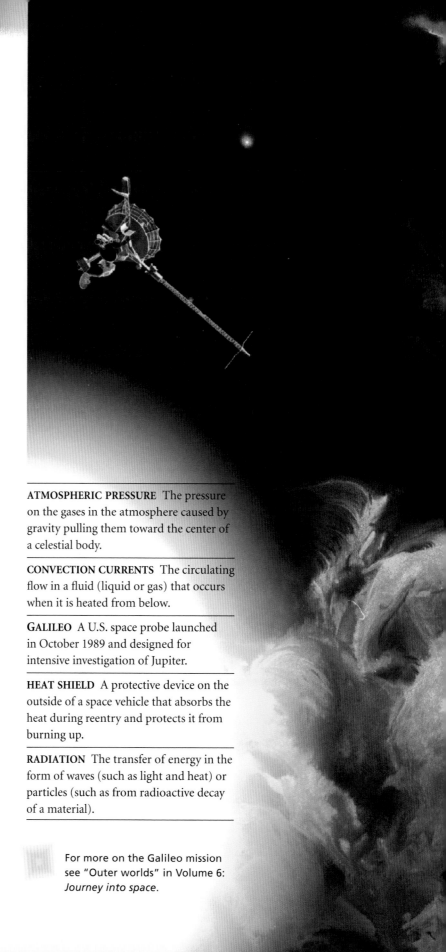

ATMOSPHERIC PRESSURE The pressure on the gases in the atmosphere caused by gravity pulling them toward the center of a celestial body.

CONVECTION CURRENTS The circulating flow in a fluid (liquid or gas) that occurs when it is heated from below.

GALILEO A U.S. space probe launched in October 1989 and designed for intensive investigation of Jupiter.

HEAT SHIELD A protective device on the outside of a space vehicle that absorbs the heat during reentry and protects it from burning up.

RADIATION The transfer of energy in the form of waves (such as light and heat) or particles (such as from radioactive decay of a material).

For more on the Galileo mission see "Outer worlds" in Volume 6: *Journey into space.*

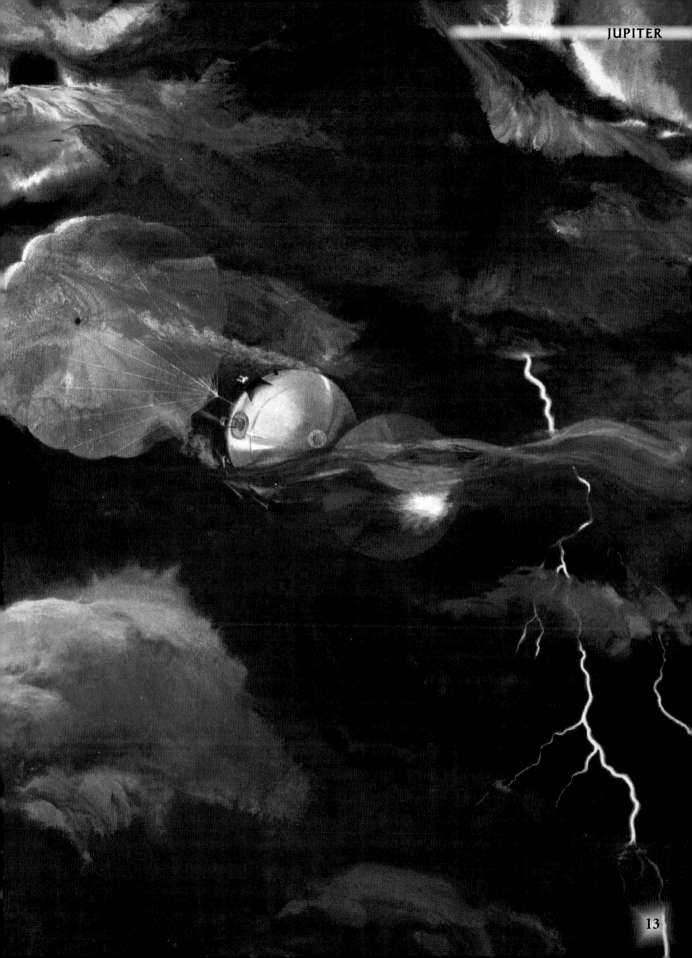

▼ This picture of the area around the Great Red Spot shows clouds of differing heights. Reddish-orange areas show high-level clouds, yellow areas show midlevel clouds, and green areas show lower-level clouds. Light blue shows ammonia ice clouds. The ammonia cloud is produced by powerful updrafts of ammonia-laden air from deep within Jupiter's atmosphere.

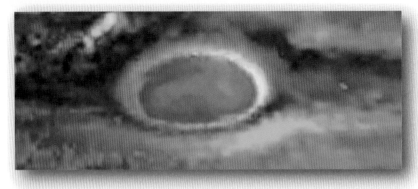

Great Red Spot

The **GREAT RED SPOT**—more pink in color than actually red—lies among the belts of moving cloud, drifting along with them, although at a slower rate. There are three large ovals south of the Great Red Spot, which are also fairly permanent features. Again, they stay at their own latitudes like the rest of the clouds.

Although the Great Red Spot is the most conspicuous part of the planet, we still have limited knowledge of what it is, and what makes it so large and so permanent.

The gases in the Great Red Spot travel counterclockwise, making a complete rotation within the spot every 12 days. If it is a large eddy, then the apparently still-looking center tells us it cannot be a region where gases are welling up. If it were, it would look much like a giant **HURRICANE** as seen from space.

Colored clouds

The clouds that we see are probably made of different substances at different heights. Just as we have tall clouds whose tops are made of ice crystals, so Jupiter appears to have tall white clouds, in this case made of frozen ammonia crystals. The brown clouds are lower and probably made of **CONDENSED** ammonium hydrosulfide, with sulfur **COMPOUNDS** providing the coloration.

▲ The Great Red Spot is still present in Jupiter's atmosphere more than 300 years after it was first observed. It is now known that it is a vast storm, spinning like a fierce anticyclone with winds inside approaching 500 km/hr.

The Great Red Spot is the largest known atmospheric system in the solar system. It is almost twice the size of the Earth and one-sixth the diameter of Jupiter.

The Red Spot changes its shape, size, and color, but not its latitude.

Jupiter is composed primarily of hydrogen and helium. Helium is an unreactive gas, and so most of the other ELEMENTS present react only with hydrogen. Thus the gas clouds are compounds that include hydrogen, methane, ammonia, and water.

The reason why water is found is that the freezing point of water falls dramatically as PRESSURE increases, and pressures in the Jovian atmosphere are far higher than on Earth.

With sulfur compounds helping color the brown clouds, what tints the Great Red Spot? No one really knows. It may be due to phosphorus, to some organic compound, or just to a different compound of sulfur.

Jupiter's magnetic field

In 1955 it was found that Jupiter sent out RADIO WAVES. This was the first time that a planet had been found to send out such RADIATION.

The EMISSIONS occur as bursts of great intensity, often more intense than emissions from the Sun.

Because radio waves and MAGNETISM are closely related, the burst of radio energy is a sign that the planet has a MAGNETIC FIELD. For the emissions to be so powerful, the magnetic field must also be hugely powerful and actively moving, just as it is on Earth.

COMPOUND A substance made from two or more elements that have chemically combined.

CONDENSE To change state from a gas or vapor to a liquid.

ELEMENT A substance that cannot be decomposed into simpler substances by chemical means.

EMISSION Something that is sent or let out.

HURRICANE A very violent cyclone that begins close to the equator, and that contains winds of over 117 km/hr.

MAGNETIC FIELD The region of influence of a magnetic body.

MAGNETISM An invisible force that has the property of attracting iron and similar metals.

MAGNETOSPHERE A region in the upper atmosphere, or around a planet, where magnetic phenomena such as auroras are found.

PRESSURE The force per unit area.

RADIATION The transfer of energy in the form of waves (such as light and heat) or particles (such as from radioactive decay of a material).

RADIO WAVES A form of electromagnetic radiation, like light and heat.

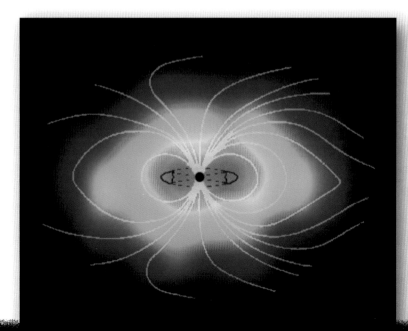

◄ A vast **MAGNETOSPHERE** of charged particles whirls around Jupiter.

The black circle shows the size of Jupiter, the lines indicate Jupiter's magnetic field, and there is also a cross section of the Io ring of charged particles that originate from volcanic eruptions on Jupiter's moon Io and circle Jupiter at about the orbit of Io.

Jupiter's magnetosphere is the largest object in the solar system. If it glowed at wavelengths visible to the eye, it would appear two to three times the size of the Sun or Moon to viewers on Earth.

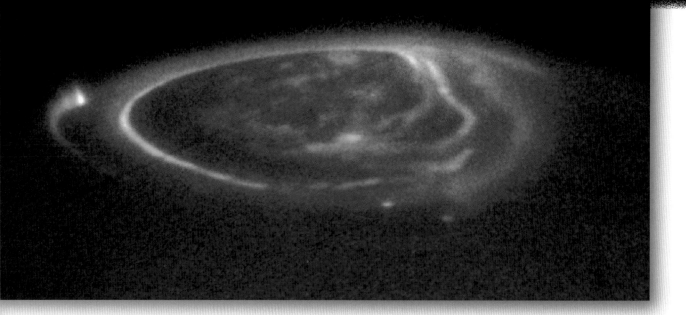

▲ This is an **ULTRAVIOLET HUBBLE SPACE TELESCOPE** closeup view of an electric-blue aurora glowing around Jupiter. The image shows the main oval of the aurora, which is centered on the magnetic north pole, plus more diffuse emissions inside the polar cap.

The Hubble image also shows emissions from the magnetic "footprints" of three of Jupiter's largest moons. Io is on the left, Ganymede is near the center, and Europa is just below and to the right of Ganymede. These emissions, produced by electric currents generated by the satellites, flow along Jupiter's magnetic field, bouncing in and out of the upper atmosphere. They are unlike anything seen on Earth.

It turns out that the magnetic field of Jupiter is 19,000 times as powerful as the Earth's magnetic field. Jupiter's magnetic field is exactly opposite that of the Earth, meaning that a compass taken from Earth would point to its south pole. But it is also worth remembering that the Earth's magnetic field flips every few hundred thousand years, so there is no reason to suppose that the Jovian magnet remains the same either.

The result of Jupiter having a magnetic field is that it experiences **AURORAS**, a phenomenon also common to the polar regions on Earth.

Jupiter's magnetic field stretches out to between the moons Europa and Ganymede. Io is in this range, and there is an invisible magnetic tube linking this moon with the planet. In this tube flows an electrical current of something like five million amps (a typical Earth lightning strike is just 20,000 amps for a fraction of a second).

Inside Jupiter

We have never seen beyond the outer regions of the Jovian atmosphere, and so we know nothing directly of the planet. But there are some things of which we can be sure: Jupiter's **CORE** is not a dead, icy rock but a searingly hot body of about 25,000°C. We know this because Jupiter sends out twice as much heat as it receives from the Sun.

From its size and **DENSITY** we can also tell what the **PRESSURE** is like in the center of this giant planet. It is probably something like 50–100 million Earth atmospheres.

We are used to hydrogen being a gas, but at this enormous pressure hydrogen turns into a substance that looks like a metal. The center of Jupiter is thus mainly metallic hydrogen. We say "mainly" because if the core were entirely hydrogen, it would have to be a lot bigger in order to explain its **MASS**. So there must be other—and heavier—elements there too. The most likely element is helium, in a ratio of about 1 part helium to 14 parts hydrogen. That is what is found in the Jovian atmosphere.

Does this metallic liquid go to the very center of Jupiter? Almost. Most people think that there is a relatively tiny solid rock core, perhaps between one and ten Earth diameters in size. Of that, however, we have no evidence at all except to say that all planets are thought to begin as rocky cores, and then some develop huge atmospheres.

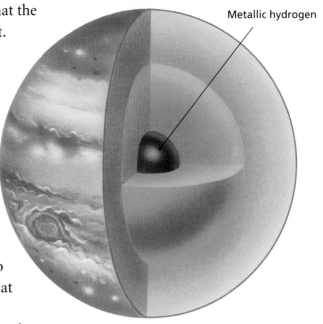

▲ The structure of Jupiter.

The formation of Jupiter

Jupiter is such a vast planet that its origin has to be very different from the other planets in the solar system. The core probably formed at an early stage by the sweeping up of dust in the solar system.

As the planet formed, gases would have been released. That provided the early atmosphere. More gas could have been pulled in from space by **GRAVITY** in much the same way as happened with the Sun. This process caused the atmosphere to get thicker and thicker.

Jupiter is almost big enough to have formed into a sun. Instead, it remains a distant, cold planet. So where does all of the heat come from? Some is perhaps left over from the time the planet formed (as on Earth), and some is perhaps produced as gases like helium condense to liquid due to the vast pressures near the core. If this were true, the explanation would be the same for Saturn.

AURORA A region of illumination, often in the form of a wavy curtain, high in the atmosphere of a planet.

CORE The central region of a body.

DENSITY A measure of the amount of matter in a space.

GRAVITY The force of attraction between bodies.

HUBBLE SPACE TELESCOPE An orbiting telescope (and so a satellite) that was placed above the Earth's atmosphere so that it could take images that were far clearer than anything that could be obtained from the surface of the Earth.

MASS The amount of matter in an object.

PRESSURE The force per unit area.

ULTRAVIOLET A form of radiation that is just beyond the violet end of the visible spectrum and so is called "ultra" (more than) violet. At the other end of the visible spectrum is "infra" (less than) red.

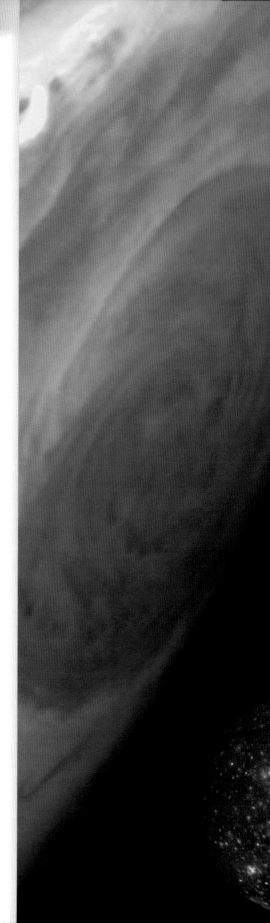

Jupiter's moons

When a probe was sent out from Earth to look at Jupiter and its moons in the mid and late 1990s, it was appropriately named **GALILEO** (see page 9). In 1610 Galileo Galilei was the first person to see the moons of Jupiter, using the newly developed telescope. The moons together are called the **GALILEAN SATELLITES** in his honor. Indeed, Galileo used the moons as another piece of evidence that the planets orbit the Sun—something that, at the time, was widely disbelieved.

Galileo saw four moons. We now call them Callisto (pages 33–34), Europa (page 29), Ganymede (pages 30–32), and Io (pages 21–26)—names associated with Jupiter in Greek mythology. We now also know there are more than these four moons. There are 16 that can be called distinct **SATELLITES**, 13 that were found by Earth observation, and three more that were discovered by **VOYAGER**.

The inner and outer moons vary in some respects. The inner eight have orbits that are nearly circular, while the outer eight have very oval orbits.

The moons of Jupiter could have developed from dust in the solar system at the same time as Jupiter did. But Jupiter had an influence on all of them. The high temperature of the growing early planet may have stopped the **CONDENSATION** of gases on the inner moons (including Io and Europa), and so they remained rocky. The outer moons (including Ganymede and Callisto), on the other hand, were in a cooler region of space; so water, for example, did not boil off into space.

The outermost eight satellites probably did not form at the same time as the inner ones, but were captured by Jupiter at a much later date.

▶ In this view the four Galilean satellites (moons) are shown to scale, although not in their correct orbital positions.

Io is closest to Jupiter, then come Europa, Ganymede, and Callisto.

Each satellite is amazingly different, even though they are relatively close to Jupiter (350,000 kilometers for Io; 1.8 million kilometers for Callisto). North is at the top of these images taken by NASA's Galileo spacecraft.

The Galilean satellites

The Galilean satellites, Io, Europa, Ganymede, and Callisto, have been an intense source of curiosity for hundreds of years. Callisto and Ganymede are as big as the planet Mercury. But it was the Voyager missions in 1979 that first showed them to be some of the most spectacular bodies in the solar system—and showed that they were each completely different and unique. Europa, for example, is coated with ice, which may cover a liquid ocean. Io is the most active volcanic body we know about in the solar system. Both Io and Europa are denser than Callisto and Ganymede. These outer bodies must be made up of at least half water.

CONDENSATION The change of state from a gas or vapor to a liquid.

GALILEAN SATELLITES The four large satellites of Jupiter discovered by astronomer Galileo Galilei in 1610. They are Callisto, Europa, Ganymede, and Io.

GALILEO A U.S. space probe launched in October 1989 and designed for intensive investigation of Jupiter.

SATELLITE An object that is in an orbit around another object, usually a planet.

VOYAGER A pair of U.S. space probes designed to provide detailed information about the outer regions of the solar system.

Io

◀ Io, the most volcanic body in the solar system, is seen in the highest resolution obtained to date by the Galileo spacecraft.

The smallest features that can be seen—rugged mountains—are 2.5 kilometers across and several kilometers high. There are also **PLATEAUS** and many irregular depressions, called volcanic **CALDERAS**.

Several of the dark, flowlike features correspond to hot spots and may be active **LAVA FLOWS**.

There are no landforms resembling impact **CRATERS**, since the vulcanism covers the surface with new deposits much more rapidly than impacting **COMETS** and **ASTEROIDS** can create new craters. The picture is centered on the side of Io that always faces away from Jupiter; north is at the top.

Until the **VOYAGER** probe (page 27) reached Io, it had seemed from Earth to be an orangy-colored moon. It is, in fact, slightly larger than the Earth's Moon, with a diameter of 3,630 km. However, it turns out to be quite unexpected in character. Thus, while Earth has an inactive Moon with a cratered surface that has remained unchanged for billions of years, Io is almost free of impact craters, which tells us that the surface renews itself in a geologically short time.

In fact, Io proves to be the most geologically active rocky body in the solar system, renewing its surface completely every few thousand years.

The orangy color seen from afar also hides the great variety of colors that adorn the surface. Since sulfur can appear in yellow, black, or red forms, it is likely that the red poles are covered in one form of sulfur, while yellow sulfur dominates nearer the equator.

ASTEROID Any of the many small objects within the solar system.

CALDERA A large pit in the top of a volcano produced when the top of the volcano explodes and collapses in on itself.

COMET A small object, often described as being like a dirty snowball, that appears to be very bright in the night sky and has a long tail when it approaches the Sun.

CRATER A deep bowl-shaped depression in the surface of a body formed by the high-speed impact of another, smaller body.

LAVA FLOW A river or sheet of liquid volcanic rock.

PLATEAU An upland plain or tableland.

VOYAGER A pair of U.S. space probes designed to provide detailed information about the outer regions of the solar system.

◀ Io is shown here as a small disk to the right of Jupiter.

Io's volcanoes

There appears to be no water on the surface of Io. The yellowish-white color is most likely frozen sulfur dioxide. The surface also has volcanic VENTS and lava flows. The LAVA flowing from these distant VOLCANOES is very hot—at least 2,000°C.

The volcano that was active at the time of the Voyager flyby has been named Prometheus. It can be seen on the full disk, page 20 (slightly right of center).

The activity on Io is all the more intriguing since Io is too small to have a source of internal heat. It has been suggested that the energy comes from the combined GRAVITATIONAL PULL of Jupiter and the other major moons, which pull and push at Io like a ball being first squeezed and then let go. Scientists call this a tidal effect; it is so powerful that it can produce intense internal heating within Io.

▼ An enormous volcanic explosion can be seen silhouetted against dark space over Io's bright LIMB.

The brightness of the plume has been increased by the computer, since it is normally extremely faint; but the relative color of the plume (greenish-white) has been preserved.

The picture shows solid material being thrown up to an altitude of about 160 km. To do this, the material must leave the volcanic vent at nearly 200 km/hr. The vent is about 300 km in diameter.

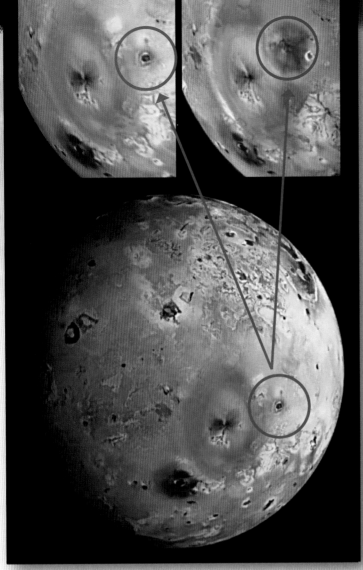

GALILEO A U.S. space probe launched in October 1989 and designed for intensive investigation of Jupiter.

GRAVITATIONAL PULL The force of attraction between bodies. The larger an object, the more its gravitational pull on other objects.

LAVA Hot, melted rock from a volcano.

LIMB The outer edge of a celestial body, including an atmosphere if it has one.

VENT A tube or fissure that allows volcanic materials to reach the surface of a planet.

VOLCANO A mound or mountain that is formed from ash or lava.

◀ These images show how rapidly the surface of Io changes. The pictures were taken 5 months apart by the **GALILEO** spacecraft. A new dark spot 400 kilometers in diameter, which is roughly the size of Arizona, surrounds a volcanic center named Pillan Patera *(right of center)*. The eruption is 120 kilometers high.

◀ This is what Io looks like using Earth-bound telescopes. The bulge on the upper right is a volcano erupting.

◀ This is a picture of Culann Patera, one of the most colorful volcanic centers on Io, as seen by the Galileo spacecraft. Culann's central caldera *(above and to the right of center)* has a highly irregular, scalloped edge and a green-colored floor. Lava flows spill out of the caldera on all sides. The loose red material around the caldera is believed to be a compound of sulfur deposited from a plume of gas.

The greenish material may be a coating of sulfur-rich material on warm lava.

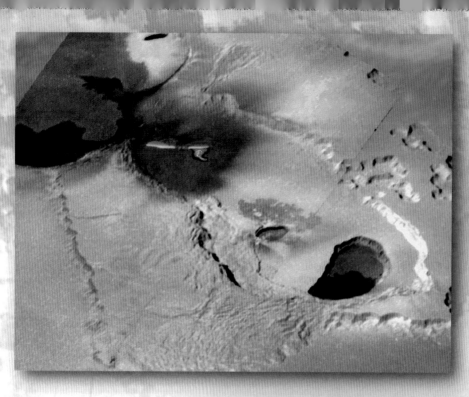

◄ An active eruption at the volcanic area called Tvashtar Catena.

▼ This diagram shows current scientific ideas about the role of sulfur in volcanoes on Io. Sulfur gas is thrown out of the hot vents (green arrow) and lands on the cold surface, where the sulfur **ATOMS** rearrange into **MOLECULES** of three or four atoms, which give the surface a red color. Eventually, the atoms rearrange into their most stable configuration, rings of eight atoms, which form ordinary pale yellow sulfur.

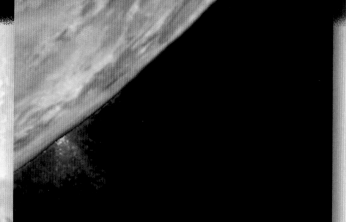

ATOM The smallest particle of an element.

MOLECULE A group of two or more atoms held together by chemical bonds.

Gas plumes on Io

◄▼ Not only does Io throw out lava as flows and as volcanoes, but it also spews mysterious plumes of gas. In these pictures a plume of gas and particles is ejected some 100 kilometers above the surface of Io. This one is named Masubi.

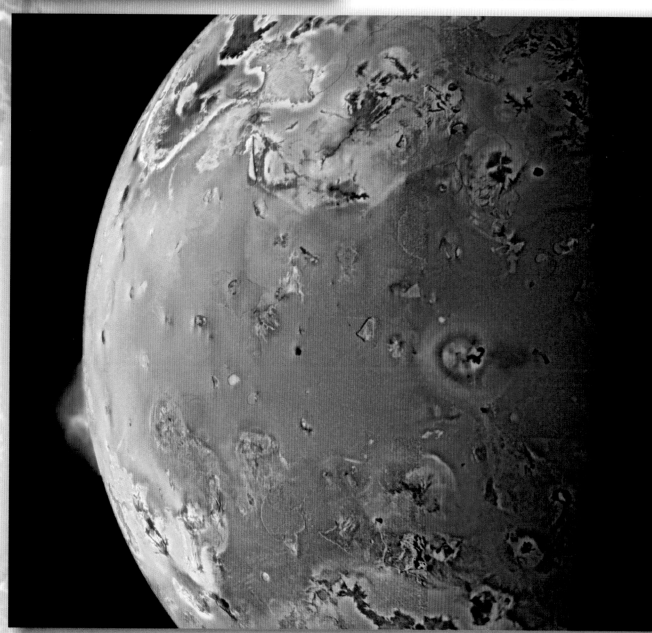

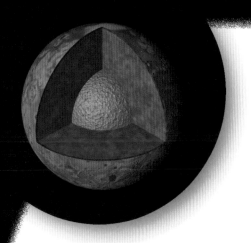

▲ The internal structure of Io. A thin crust covers a molten sulfurous mantle and an iron core.

Io spins on its **AXIS** once every 1.8 Earth days, which is the same as the length of time it takes to go around Jupiter. As a result, it always keeps the same face to Jupiter (called **SYNCHRONOUS ROTATION**).

Io has a nearly circular **ORBIT**, about 422,000 km from the center of Jupiter. The **DENSITY** of Io is 3.5 g/cm³, which suggests it is a rocky rather than a gaseous body.

It has a thin, transparent **ATMOSPHERE** made mainly of sulfur dioxide. It is believed that the source of the lava is a **MOLTEN MANTLE** below the **CRUST**, and below it is a **CORE** of molten iron and iron sulfide some 1,800 km in diameter.

Io's volcanic plumes generate particles that are pulled into Jupiter's **MAGNETIC FIELD**, creating a tube of **IONIZED** particles.

For more on Voyager see "Outer worlds" in Volume 6: *Journey into space.*

Voyager

▶ Voyager is the space probe that captured the first spectacular images of Io, Europa, Ganymede, and other parts of the Jovian system.

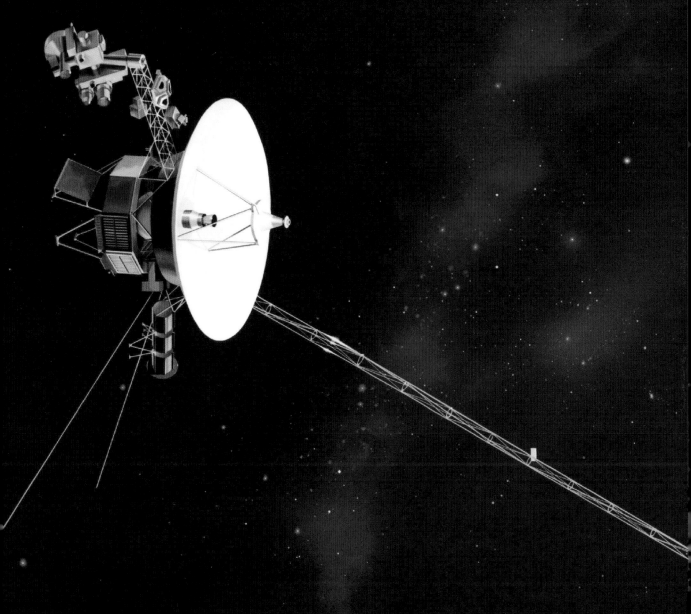

Europa

Europa, the fourth largest of Jupiter's moons, is 3,138 km across and orbits some 671,000 km from Jupiter. Its DENSITY of 3 g/cm³ suggests that it is mainly made of rock with an icy surface.

Europa has a smooth, uncratered surface. As on Io, this suggests that the surface is recent. In this case it would appear that the water under the ice must pour out onto the surface from time to time, spreading out and then refreezing.

The dark lines, thousands of kilometers long, appear to form a net stretching across Europa's surface. It is possible that they could be cracks in the rock below the ice.

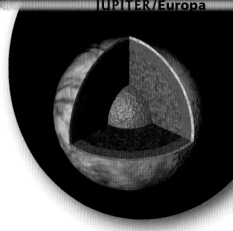

▲ Europa's metallic (iron, nickel) CORE, shown in gray, is thought to be surrounded by shells of water in ice or liquid form (shown in blue and white).

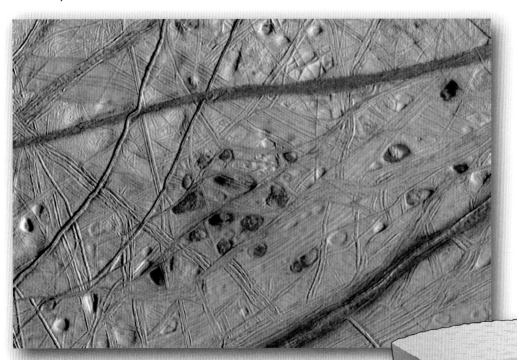

CORE The central region of a body.

DENSITY A measure of the amount of matter in a space.

▼ Evidence has shown that Europa may have a deep melted ocean under its icy shell.

◀ The Minos Linea region on Jupiter's moon Europa.

The imaging shows up the translucent nature of the icy surface of the moon, with brown and red lines in the ice. The area covered is about 1,260 km across.

▲ The spots and pits visible in this region of Europa's northern hemisphere are each about 10 km across. The dark spots are called lenticulae (Latin for freckles). Their similar sizes and spacing suggest that Europa's icy shell may be churning away like a lava lamp, with warmer ice moving upward from the bottom of the ice shell, while colder ice near the surface sinks downward. These lenticulae may hold clues to the composition of a possible ocean under the surface and to whether it could support life.

CORE The central region of a body.

CRATER A deep bowl-shaped depression in the surface of a body formed by the high-speed impact of another, smaller body.

DENSITY A measure of the amount of matter in a space.

LATITUDE Angular distance north or south of the equator, measured through 90°.

Ganymede

Ganymede, the third moon from Jupiter, is also the largest. It is bigger than the planets Mercury and Pluto, and bigger than Saturn's largest moon, Titan.

It is about 5,260 km across and orbits Jupiter at a distance of about 1.1 million kilometers. It has quite a low **DENSITY**—about 1.7 g/cm³—which suggests it may be about half water and half rock. From this point of view it is similar to Callisto. However, unlike Callisto, Ganymede was big enough to generate its own central source of heat, so that it became differentiated into a **CORE** of rock surrounded by water, with a deep "crust" of ice. Callisto appears to be still a mixture of ice and rock.

Ganymede has a surface that is partly dark and partly light. The darker regions are much more cratered, suggesting that they have been geologically inactive for far longer than the light regions have. The **CRATERS** are areas of very low relief when compared, for example, with the craters on Earth's Moon. That may be due to the fact that the ice-rich rims of craters subside under their own weight.

▶ In this global view of Ganymede's trailing side in enhanced color you can see frosty polar caps in addition to bright, grooved land and older, dark, furrowed areas.

The violet hues at the poles may be the result of small particles of frost, which would scatter more light at shorter wavelengths (the violet end of the spectrum).

Compared to Earth's polar caps, Ganymede's polar landscape is extensive, with frost on Ganymede reaching **LATITUDES** as low as 40° on average and 25° at some locations.

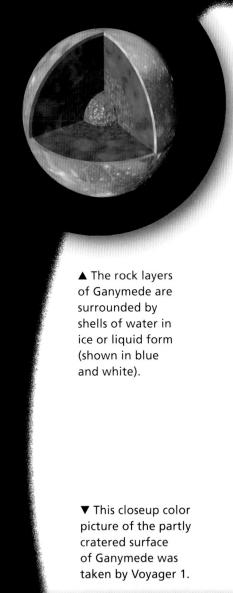

▲ The rock layers of Ganymede are surrounded by shells of water in ice or liquid form (shown in blue and white).

▼ This closeup color picture of the partly cratered surface of Ganymede was taken by Voyager 1.

The light regions look like cracked ice. The grooves that crisscross these regions are hundreds of meters deep and hundreds of kilometers long. They may be places where the ice has been cracked apart, perhaps by the churning motion of the ocean below. Any cracks formed in the ice would soon be frozen over.

Ganymede is the only moon known to have a **MAGNETOSPHERE**, or region of **MAGNETISM**. Again, it is likely that it is made by **CONVECTION CURRENTS** churning over in a metal/rock core. Ganymede's and Jupiter's magnetospheres interact, producing spectacular **AURORAS**.

Ganymede's **MAGNETIC FIELD** may be partly responsible for the appearance of the polar landscape.

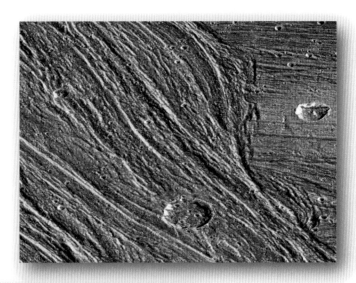

▲ Complex sets of ridges and grooves in the Nippur Sulcus region on Ganymede. The large crater at the bottom is about 12 kilometers in diameter.

Callisto

Of its largest moons, Callisto is the furthest from Jupiter. The moon is 4,800 km across and orbits about 1.8 million km from Jupiter.

Compared with Io and Europa, the surface of Callisto appears dark. Also, unlike the inner moons, Callisto's surface is heavily marked with impact **CRATERS**, somewhat like Earth's Moon. This suggests that Callisto is geologically inactive and has been so since the early stages of the development of the solar system.

AURORA A region of illumination, often in the form of a wavy curtain, high in the atmosphere of a planet.

CONVECTION CURRENTS The circulating flow in a fluid (liquid or gas) that occurs when it is heated from below.

CRATER A deep bowl-shaped depression in the surface of a body formed by the high-speed impact of another, smaller body.

MAGNETIC FIELD The region of influence of a magnetic body.

MAGNETISM An invisible force that has the property of attracting iron and similar metals.

MAGNETOSPHERE A region in the upper atmosphere, or around a planet, where magnetic phenomena such as auroras are found.

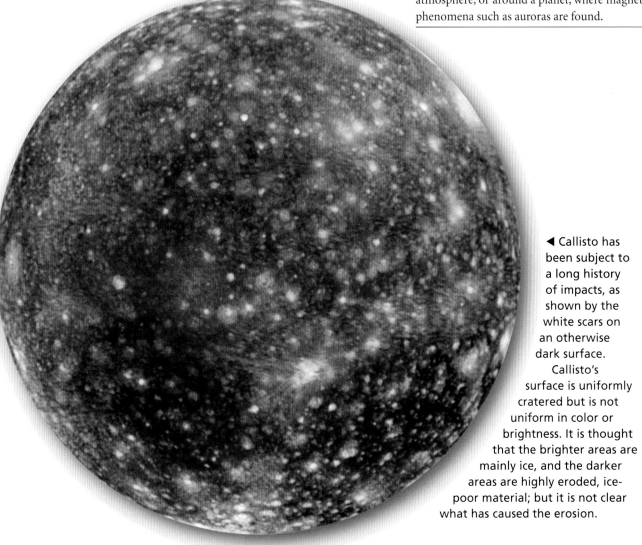

◀ Callisto has been subject to a long history of impacts, as shown by the white scars on an otherwise dark surface. Callisto's surface is uniformly cratered but is not uniform in color or brightness. It is thought that the brighter areas are mainly ice, and the darker areas are highly eroded, ice-poor material; but it is not clear what has caused the erosion.

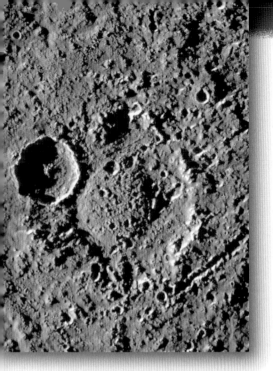

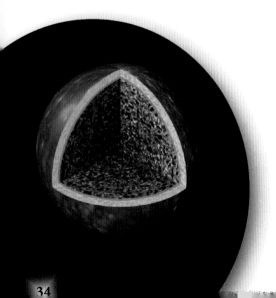

Callisto has a low **DENSITY**—just $1.83\,\mathrm{g/cm^3}$. This is a density that would occur if the moon were about half rock and half ice. However, ice is not common on the surface. If ice does exist, therefore, it must all be mixed up with the rock (as it is, for example, in **COMETS**).

Many of the craters are some tens of kilometers across, but some are multiringed craters measuring hundreds of kilometers in diameter. However, unlike the Earth's Moon, Callisto has almost no surface relief, possibly because the rims of the craters (being made of a mixture of ice and rock) melted down shortly after they were produced.

The dark surface coloring may possibly include material containing carbon.

The smaller satellites

The force that makes all stars, planets, and moons into **SPHERES** is **GRAVITY**. Gravity varies with the **MASS** of the body. For gravity to be powerful enough to pull the material into a sphere, the body has to be quite large. Io, Ganymede, Europa, and Callisto are spheres because they are big enough to have a strong gravity. But the other satellites are so small that gravity cannot pull their rocks into spheres, and so they remain potato-shaped chunks of planetary debris moving in space. Most likely, they have been trapped by Jupiter's gravity and then have moved into orbit rather than crashing into the planet.

▲ A heavily cratered region near Callisto's equator. The 50-kilometer double-ring crater in the center is named Har. Har has an unusual rounded mound on its floor. The origin of the mound is unclear, but it probably involves uplift of ice-rich materials from below.

▼ Callisto is considered to be a relatively uniform mixture of comparable amounts of ice and rock.

Jupiter's moons and rings

▶ The innermost and thickest ring, shown in gray shading, is the halo that ends at the main ring.

The thin, narrow main ring, shown with red shading, is bounded by the 16-kilometer-wide satellite Adrastea and shows a marked decrease in brightness near the orbit of Jupiter's innermost moon, Metis. It is composed of fine particles knocked off Adrastea and Metis.

Impacts by small meteoroids into these small, low-gravity satellites feed material into the rings.

Thebe and Amalthea, the next two satellites in increasing distance from Jupiter, supply the dust that forms the thicker filmlike rings. These filmy rings are shown with yellow and green shading.

Some of the satellites move in the same direction as Jupiter's **ROTATION**, for example, Leda, Himalia, Lysithea, and Elara, while others move against the direction of rotation, for example, Ananke, Carme, Pasiphae, and Sinope.

Jupiter's ring system

Until Voyager 1 approached Jupiter, no one knew for certain that the planet had a ring system orbiting around it. We now know that the ring system is made up of billions of dust-sized particles that show up because of the way they scatter sunlight, producing a kind of halo effect.

It is likely that the particles of the ring are produced by **METEOROIDS** crashing on the surface of Io, scattering debris into space, and also possibly by particles ejected from Io's **VOLCANOES**.

COMET A small object, often described as being like a dirty snowball, that appears to be very bright in the night sky and has a long tail when it approaches the Sun.

DENSITY A measure of the amount of matter in a space.

GRAVITY The force of attraction between bodies.

MASS The amount of matter in an object.

METEOROID A small body moving in the solar system that becomes a meteor if it enters the Earth's atmosphere.

ROTATION Spinning around an axis.

SPHERE A ball-shaped object.

VOLCANO A mound or mountain that is formed from ash or lava.

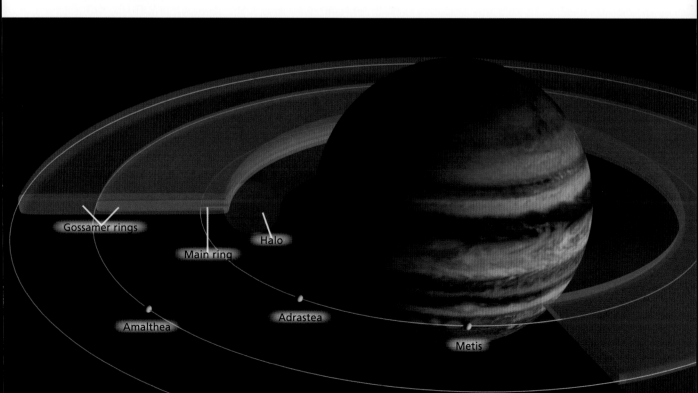

Gossamer rings

Main ring

Halo

Amalthea

Adrastea

Metis

▲ This view of the Saturnian system was prepared by putting together images taken by the **VOYAGER** 1 spacecraft during its Saturn encounter in November 1980. Dione is in the forefront, Saturn rising behind, Tethys and Mimas fading in the distance to the right, Enceladus and Rhea off Saturn's rings to the left, and Titan in its distant orbit at the top.

3: SATURN

Saturn is the second largest of the planets and sixth farthest from the Sun. Saturn **ORBITS** the Sun at a distance of about 1.4 billion km.

Saturn is the planet with the most distinctive rings in the whole solar system. If Saturn and its rings were placed between the Earth and the Moon, they would barely fit. The distance between the Earth and the Moon is 384,400 kilometers, while the diameter of the A-ring (see page 44) outer edge measures 273,550 kilometers.

◀ An artist's impression of Cassini, the latest of the space **PROBES** to investigate Saturn.

For more on Cassini see "Outer worlds" in Volume 6: *Journey into space.*

ATMOSPHERE The envelope of gases that surrounds the Earth and other bodies in the universe.

AXIS (pl. **AXES**) The line around which a body spins.

CORE The central region of a body.

DENSITY A measure of the amount of matter in a space.

MAGNETIC FIELD The region of influence of a magnetic body.

MASS The amount of matter in an object.

MATTER Anything that exists in physical form.

ORBIT The path followed by one object as it tracks around another.

PROBE An unmanned spacecraft designed to explore our solar system and beyond.

STAR A large ball of gases that radiates light. The star nearest the Earth is the Sun.

VOYAGER A pair of U.S. space probes designed to provide detailed information about the outer regions of the solar system.

The most striking rings that encircle Saturn can be seen clearly on Earth because, like the Earth, Saturn is noticeably tilted on its **AXIS**. In the case of Saturn the tilt is 26.7° (that of the Earth is 23.5°).

Saturn spins quite quickly on its axis, making a complete turn in about 10 hours, that is, in less than half an Earth day. However, Saturn takes 29.4 Earth years to revolve around the Sun.

Interestingly, Saturn is nearly the same size as Jupiter, although it has only a third of Jupiter's **MASS**. In fact, Saturn is the least dense of all of the planets, with a **DENSITY** of just 0.7 g/cm³ (that is, it would float on water). So, although Saturn is 766 times as big as the Earth, it "weighs" (its mass is) just 95 times that of the Earth.

Saturn is another of the planets that, with Jupiter, had all the makings of a **STAR** but never developed into one, probably because there was never enough space **MATTER** in its orbit to allow it to grow to a critical size.

The core

It is very difficult to find out much about the planet's interior because of its immensely thick **ATMOSPHERE**. But it is known to have a **MAGNETIC FIELD**, and so near the **CORE** there must be a moving body of metal.

Gas

Metallic core

Dust bands

Liquid

▶ The suggested structure of Saturn.

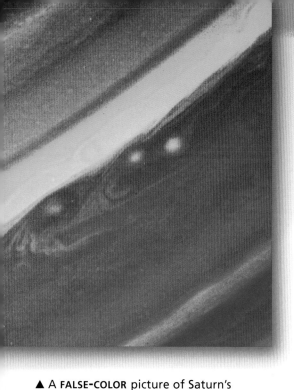

The core of Saturn is made of 50% hydrogen. But at the huge **PRESSURES** existing in the center of the planet, the hydrogen changes from a liquid and becomes a liquid metal (to imagine this, think of the silvery metal mercury). At the very core there may well be a mixture of rock and ice of up to 20 times the mass of the Earth.

The churning over of the liquid metallic hydrogen near the core is responsible for the magnetic field. Saturn's magnetic field is similar to that of the Earth, resembling a giant bar magnet. The magnetic field lines up almost exactly with the geographical north and south **POLES** and is not offset, as on the Earth.

Like Jupiter, Saturn radiates more heat to space than it receives from the Sun, and so it must have a hot core.

The fact that Saturn has no solid surface makes it difficult to say how big the planet is. The diameter of the planet is usually taken to be about 121,000 km.

▲ A **FALSE-COLOR** picture of Saturn's northern hemisphere. There are several weather patterns visible. Two spots are flowing westward at about 15 meters per second. The third, most westerly, spot has a cloud system that is part of this westward flow, although the spot itself is flowing east at about 30 meters per second. The ribbonlike feature to the north marks a high-speed flow of air where wind speeds approach 150 meters per second.

Saturn is not a precise sphere but is flattened on both poles. Its pole-to-pole diameter is 10% less than its diameter at the **EQUATOR**. This is the result of **CENTRIFUGAL FORCE** throwing the gases of the planet outward against **GRAVITY** more strongly at the equator than at the poles.

The atmosphere

Saturn's **ATMOSPHERE** is 91% hydrogen, more in percentage terms than any other planet in the solar system. Helium makes up just 6%, with smaller amounts of methane and ammonia.

In the inner regions of the atmosphere the pressure is equal to millions of Earth's atmospheres, and hydrogen turns into a liquid. On the other hand, the pressure also causes the temperature of the inner atmosphere to be several thousand degrees.

ATMOSPHERE The envelope of gases that surrounds the Earth and other bodies in the universe.

CENTRIFUGAL FORCE A force that acts on an orbiting or spinning body, tending to oppose gravity and move away from the center of rotation.

EQUATOR The ring drawn around a body midway between the poles.

FALSE COLOR The colors used to make the appearance of some property more obvious.

GRAVITY The force of attraction between bodies.

LATITUDE Angular distance north or south of the equator, measured through 90°.

MASS The amount of matter in an object.

POLE The geographic pole is the place where a line drawn along the axis of rotation exits from a body's surface.

PRESSURE The force per unit area.

◄ This false-color image of Saturn provides detailed information on the clouds and hazes in Saturn's atmosphere.

The blue colors indicate a clear atmosphere down to a main cloud layer.

Different shadings of blue indicate variations in the cloud particles in size or chemical composition. The cloud particles are believed to be ammonia-ice crystals. The dark region around the south pole at the bottom indicates a big hole in the main cloud layer.

The green and yellow colors indicate a haze above the main cloud layer.

The haze is thin where the colors are green but thick where they are yellow. Most of the southern hemisphere (the lower part of Saturn) is quite hazy. These layers are aligned with **LATITUDE** lines due to Saturn's east-west winds.

The red and orange colors indicate clouds reaching up high into the atmosphere.

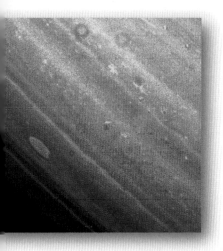

▲ This false-color image shows that Saturn also has a red spot. False color has been used to make the faint spot more visible.

Saturn does not have an atmosphere with clouds of liquid water as on Earth. Instead, its uppermost clouds are made from tiny crystals of solid ammonia. Lower down there may be crystals of ammonium hydrosulfide and, below this, water-ice crystals.

The yellow color of the clouds (and hence the yellow appearance of the planet when seen with telescopes) is thought to be due to phosphorus **COMPOUNDS** within the clouds.

The moons and rings

Saturn has more **SATELLITES** than any other planet in the solar system. Some of them are large enough to be called moons and to have names. The others are simply named by using S followed by a number. There are 18 named satellites and a dozen with letter-number labels. Each of the distinctive rings is named by using the letters from A (see pages 44–45).

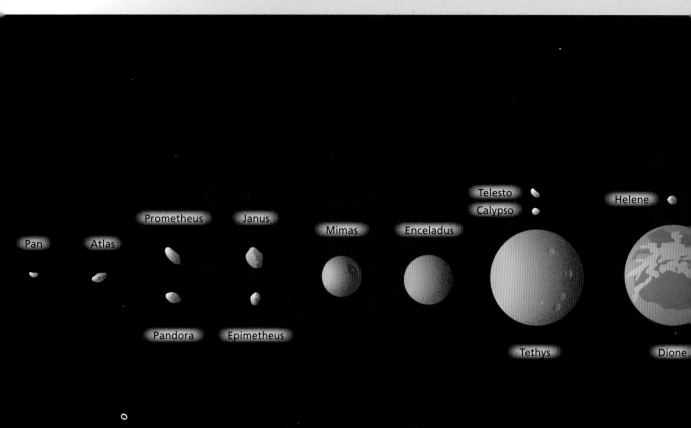

Pan Atlas Prometheus Pandora Janus Epimetheus Mimas Enceladus Telesto Calypso Tethys Helene Dione

Some of the satellites appear to control the way the rings behave. They are known as **SHEPHERD SATELLITES**. For example, the F-ring is shepherded by satellites S15 and S16. Many of the satellites interact, sharing **MOMENTUM** and influencing one another's orbits. All of the satellites are also influenced by Saturn itself, which pulls them into circular orbits.

Titan

Titan is the largest of the moons that orbit Saturn. It is also the only moon in the solar system known to have a dense atmosphere. In Titan's case the atmosphere is made of nitrogen with about 10% methane (the Earth's atmosphere is nitrogen with about 20% oxygen and small amounts of other gases).

COMPOUND A substance made from two or more elements that have chemically combined.

MOMENTUM The mass of an object multiplied by its velocity.

SATELLITE An object that is in an orbit around another object, usually a planet.

SHEPHERD SATELLITES Larger natural satellites that have an influence on small debris in nearby rings because of their gravity.

TOPOGRAPHY The shape of the land surface in terms of height.

▼ All of the main satellites are to scale except for Pan, Atlas, Telesto, Calypso, and Helene, whose sizes have been exaggerated by a factor of five to show rough **TOPOGRAPHY**.

Rhea

Titan

Hyperion

Iapetus

Phoebe

Within this atmosphere there are dense clouds that appear brown and permanently obscure the solid surface of the moon—perhaps as a result of the reaction of sunlight with particles containing carbon or nitrogen, producing a natural **PHOTOCHEMICAL SMOG**.

Mimas

This moon has a highly cratered surface. It includes the Herschel Crater, which is 130 km across and is proportionally one of the largest **CRATERS** of any body in the solar system.

Normally, impacts to produce craters of this size would have brought about the disintegration of the moon, so it is not clear what saved Mimas from destruction.

Enceladus

This moon is very **REFLECTIVE** and looks white. It also seems to have been geologically active and may have **VOLCANOES** (see bottom picture on pages 6–7).

Tethys

This is a large but geologically inactive moon. It has a heavily cratered surface of low relief, which shows no signs of having changed since early in the history of the solar system. It may be a mixture of rock and ice, which would have allowed crater rims to have slumped down, rather than staying elevated as they are on the Earth's Moon.

Dione

This is another moon that shows signs that it may have been geologically active. Its heavily cratered surface is split by fissures, and some **PLAINS** appear to have been resurfaced by **LAVA**.

Iapetus

This is a strange moon—half dark, half light. The light half appears to be icy, but the cause of the dark surface remains unknown.

▲ The moon Titan, enveloped in perpetual cloud.

▲ The moon Mimas, with its extraordinary Herschel Crater.

CRATER A deep bowl-shaped depression in the surface of a body formed by the high-speed impact of another, smaller body.

LAVA Hot, melted rock from a volcano.

PHOTOCHEMICAL SMOG A hazy atmosphere, often brown, resulting from the reaction of nitrogen gases with sunlight.

PLAIN A flat or gently rolling part of a landscape.

REFLECTIVE To bounce back any light that falls on a surface.

VOLCANO A mound or mountain that is formed from ash or lava.

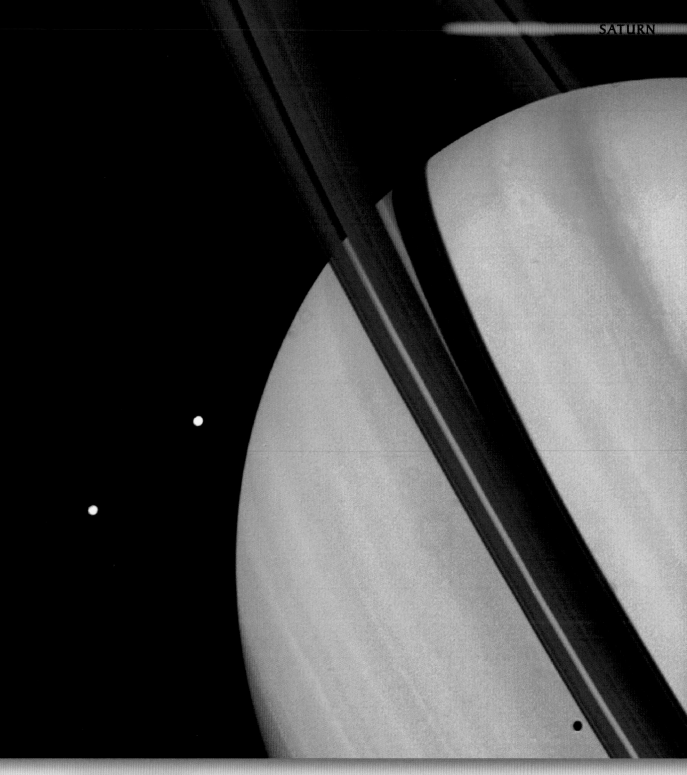

◄ The mysterious
half-dark, half-light
moon Iapetus.

▲ Saturn and two of its moons, Tethys
(above) and Dione. The shadows of
Saturn's three bright rings and Tethys
are cast onto the cloud tops.

▲ Possible variations in chemical composition from one part of Saturn's ring system to another are visible in this enhanced color picture.

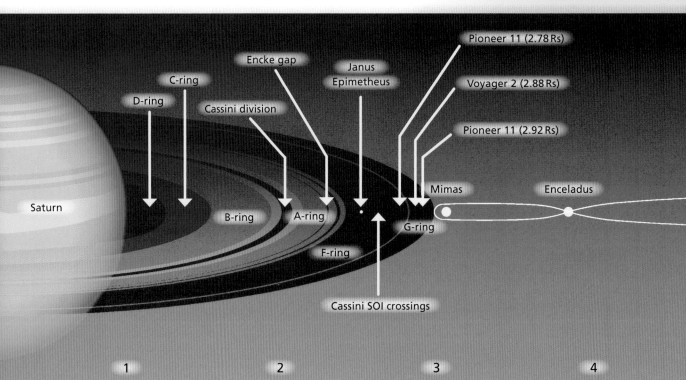

Pioneer 11 (2.78 Rs)

Voyager 2 (2.88 Rs)

Pioneer 11 (2.92 Rs)

Encke gap

C-ring

D-ring

Janus
Epimetheus

Cassini division

Mimas

Enceladus

Saturn

B-ring

A-ring

G-ring

F-ring

Cassini SOI crossings

1

2

3

4

The rings

When people think of Saturn, they immediately think of its spectacular rings.

The rings are just over 270,000 km across but only between 100 m and 1 km thick. In total, this filmy feature contains less **MATTER** than the single moon of Mimas.

Each ring is made from myriad tiny ice and rock particles, and the rings are separated by gaps.

The rings mainly lie within a distance approximately equal to Saturn's diameter. At this closeness to the planet the immense **GRAVITY** of Saturn prevents the tiny rock fragments from grouping to make new moons. At the same time, if any large moon entered into this zone, it would be torn apart by Saturn's gravity and made into more fragments for the rings. This may explain the rings—they are made of the debris, both rock and ice, created when larger moons were torn apart.

The rings were divided by observers on Earth into A, B, and (fainter) C rings, but the **VOYAGER** spacecraft missions showed that there were more rings.

GRAVITY The force of attraction between bodies.

MATTER Anything that exists in physical form.

RADIUS (pl. **RADII**) The distance from the center to the outside of a circle or sphere.

VOYAGER A pair of U.S. space probes designed to provide detailed information about the outer regions of the solar system.

▼ The rings of Saturn. The units are Saturn **RADII** (Rs), which are a unit of distance equivalent to the **RADIUS** (half the diameter) of Saturn. One Saturn radius is approximately 60,500 km.

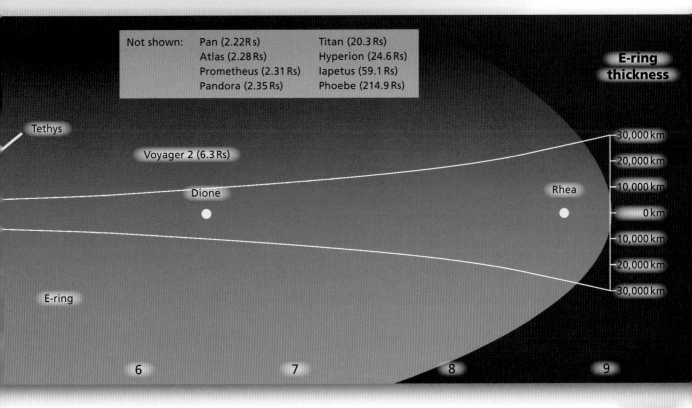

Not shown:
Pan (2.22 Rs)
Atlas (2.28 Rs)
Prometheus (2.31 Rs)
Pandora (2.35 Rs)
Titan (20.3 Rs)
Hyperion (24.6 Rs)
Iapetus (59.1 Rs)
Phoebe (214.9 Rs)

E-ring thickness

Tethys

Voyager 2 (6.3 Rs)

Dione

Rhea

30,000 km
20,000 km
10,000 km
0 km
10,000 km
20,000 km
30,000 km

E-ring

6   7   8   9

Farthest from the planet is the E-ring. It extends from 3 to 8 Saturn radii. Inside it is the G-ring, at 2.8 Saturn radii, which shows up only faintly even from close views such as taken by the Voyager spacecraft. Then comes the narrow, shepherded F-ring at 2.33 Saturn radii.

The outermost main ring is the A-ring. It stretches from 2.32 to 2.02 Saturn radii. Within it is the **ENCKE GAP** (2.21 Saturn radii) and the **KEELER GAP** (2.26 Saturn radii). The A-ring is separated from the B-ring by a zone with few particles in it called the Cassini division (1.95 to 2.02 Saturn radii). The B-ring is the thickest and broadest of the rings, extending from 1.52 to 1.95 Saturn radii. Within it is the Huygens gap (1.95 Saturn radii). The C-ring (also called the Crepe ring) lies between 1.23 and 1.52 Saturn radii. Within it is the Maxwell gap (1.45 Saturn radii). Inside it the D-ring (1.11 to 1.23 Saturn radii) is visible only in reflected light.

Many of the gaps and even some of the rings have only been known about since spacecraft exploration.

It is believed that the **GRAVITATIONAL FIELD** of a moon about 10 km across will keep a gap open. One such moon (S18) is found in the Encke gap. Gaps can also be formed by **SHEPHERD SATELLITES**. For example, the outer edge of the B-ring is shepherded by Mimas. The outer edge of the A-ring is shepherded by Janus.

ENCKE GAP A gap between rings around Saturn named for the astronomer Johann Franz Encke (1791–1865).

GRAVITATIONAL FIELD The region surrounding a body in which that body's gravitational force can be felt.

KEELER GAP A gap in the rings of Saturn named for the astronomer James Edward Keeler (1857–1900).

SHEPHERD SATELLITES Larger natural satellites that have an influence on small debris in nearby rings because of their gravity.

▶ This view, which shows Saturn's C-ring (and also the B-ring at top and left) was compiled from Voyager 2. More than 60 bright and dark ringlets can be seen. C-ring material is gray-blue, the color of dirty ice. Color differences between this ring and the B-ring indicate differences in composition of the material of the two rings.

4: URANUS

Uranus is the seventh planet farthest from the Sun. It is accompanied by numerous **SATELLITES**, including five moons. In addition, it has ten narrow rings.

Uranus **ORBITS** the Sun at a distance of 2.8 billion km, spinning on its **AXIS** in a clockwise direction, the opposite of Earth. A Uranian day is 17.24 Earth hours.

The orbit takes 84 Earth years. Thus, although the change between day and night is very rapid, the change between "summer" and "winter" takes 42 years on Uranus.

Uranus is unusual in that it spins on its side when compared to its orbit around the Sun. This is thought to be due to an ancient collision during the formation of the planets that knocked Uranus on its side.

Uranus has a low **DENSITY** (1.3 g/cm³) and is four times the diameter of the Earth (51,800 km), roughly the same size as Neptune. However, this is far smaller than the two giant planets, Jupiter and Saturn.

Unlike the Earth, Uranus has little solid rock. It is mainly made from hydrogen, helium, and water.

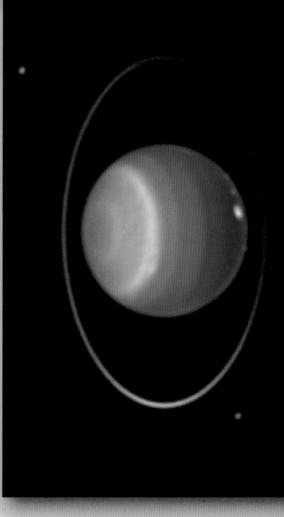

▲ Uranus with its moons.

▼ Uranus seen in true color seems to be a uniformly greenish-blue planet (*left*); but when seen in **FALSE COLOR**, the differences in latitudinal cloud bands show through clearly (*right*).

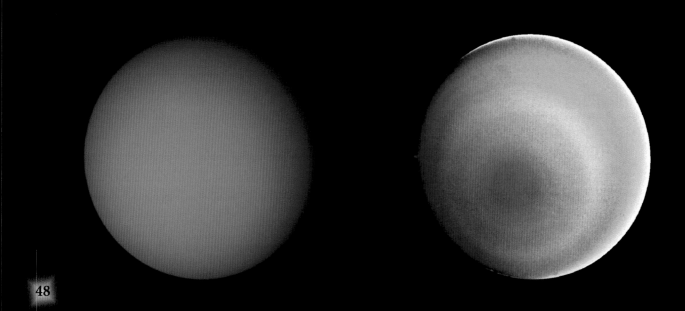

Although methane makes up only 2.3% of the Uranian **ATMOSPHERE**, the gas strongly absorbs red light. As a result, the planet **REFLECTS** only the **COMPLEMENTARY COLOR** from the color spectrum. That is why it looks blue-green.

Uranus has a **MAGNETIC FIELD** that is positioned in a quite different place than the geographic **POLES**, some 58° relative to the axis on which it spins.

As on Saturn, the **ROTATION** of the planet causes **CENTRIFUGAL FORCES** to pull the gases away from a truly spherical (ball-like) shape, so that it is slightly flattened (by 2.2%) at the poles.

How can the composition of Uranus be explained? Because it doesn't have a rock **CORE** (or if it does, it is very small), it is unlikely to have captured gas to itself by **GRAVITY** like the other planets. Rather, it seems to be the case that rocky and ice materials were captured by a planet that was made up of a ball of gases.

The atmosphere

Uranus has a thick atmosphere made up primarily of hydrogen and helium. There is a greater proportion of helium in the Uranian atmosphere than on Saturn or Jupiter. The lower part of the atmosphere also contains water, ammonia, and hydrogen sulfide.

The Uranian atmosphere is almost featureless, although winds are strong, and gases move in parallel bands. They were faintly detected in visits by the **VOYAGER** spacecraft. However, although winds reach over 200 m/s, Uranus does not appear to be a stormy planet like Saturn or Jupiter.

ATMOSPHERE The envelope of gases that surrounds the Earth and other bodies in the universe.

AXIS (pl. **AXES**) The line around which a body spins.

CENTRIFUGAL FORCE A force that acts on an orbiting or spinning body, tending to oppose gravity and move away from the center of rotation.

COMPLEMENTARY COLOR A color that is diametrically opposite another in the range, or circle, of colors in the spectrum; for example, cyan (blue) is the complement of red.

CORE The central region of a body.

DENSITY A measure of the amount of matter in a space.

FALSE COLOR The colors used to make the appearance of some property more obvious.

GRAVITY The force of attraction between bodies.

MAGNETIC FIELD The region of influence of a magnetic body.

ORBIT The path followed by one object as it tracks around another.

POLE The geographic pole is the place where a line drawn along the axis of rotation exits from a body's surface.

REFLECT To bounce back any light that falls on a surface.

ROTATION Spinning around an axis.

SATELLITE An object that is in orbit around another object, usually a planet.

VOYAGER A pair of U.S. space probes designed to provide detailed information about the outer regions of the solar system.

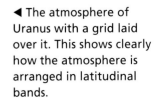

◄ The atmosphere of Uranus with a grid laid over it. This shows clearly how the atmosphere is arranged in latitudinal bands.

The core

At the center of the planet the **PRESSURE** is about five million Earth atmospheres. However, the **GRAVITATIONAL FIELD** is still not enough to make the core solid. Thus, although rock and ice probably make up 80% of the total **MASS** of Uranus, they are likely to be well mixed with gases and not concentrated at the core. In fact, it is likely that Uranus has very little rocky core at all.

Uranus is the only one of the giant planets not to radiate significantly more energy than it receives. Nevertheless, it actually sends out about the same amount of heat as it absorbs, making the **RADIATION** 10,000 times more than Earth (whose small mass lost most of its heat long ago).

The heat of Uranus was probably first created when the planet began to gather its mass of gas and concentrate it. Because Uranus is so huge, it was able to store the heat, although apparently less well than Jupiter and Saturn. As a result, its core is now much colder than those of its bigger neighbors.

The **MAGNETIC FIELD** that spreads out from Uranus is a result of the churning over of liquids below the gaseous surface. In this case it is thought that the **MAGNETISM** is generated relatively close to the surface. As the charged particles of the magnetic field interact with the **SOLAR WIND**, they generate an **AURORA**. It stretches out behind the planet in the form of a corkscrewlike tail.

Satellites and rings

Uranus has at least 22 **SATELLITES**, of which the five largest can be called moons. The four largest satellites are Ariel, Umbriel, Titania, and Oberon. Most of the smaller ones were discovered by the Voyager spacecraft missions.

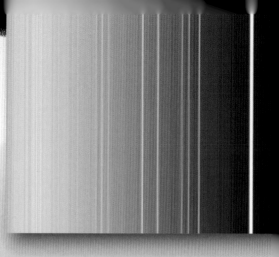

▲ The filmy rings of Uranus are shown by these lines.

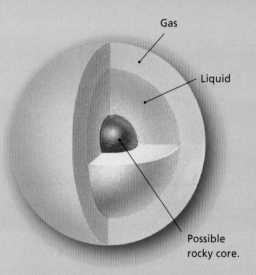

Gas

Liquid

Possible rocky core.

▲ A suggested structure of Uranus. The rocky core may be nonexistent or very small.

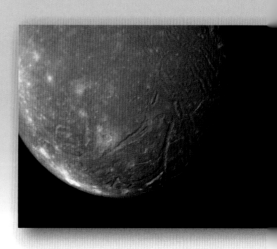

▶ The moon Ariel, showing the riftlike features that suggest it may have been geologically active at one time.

Each satellite has a density that suggests they are about 60% ice and 40% rock. Miranda and the smaller satellites are less dense and so must have a higher ice content. The surfaces of all satellites appear to consist of dirty water-ice.

Oberon and Umbriel have surfaces that are greatly marked with impact **CRATERS**, suggesting they formed at an early stage in the evolution of the solar system. By contrast, Titania and Ariel have relatively few craters and are thought to be much younger, although there is no convincing explanation for this as yet.

Large cracks appear on all of the satellites, especially Miranda, where they are up to 80 kilometers wide and 15 kilometers deep. The cracking of the crust may not be due to any geological activity inside the satellites, but rather more probably due to the original liquid core freezing and so expanding as it turned to ice. But again there is no convincing theory to explain how water could once have existed in liquid form in such cold parts of the solar system.

The rings were not discovered until 1977. They are made of a dark, sootlike material, with boulders a meter or more across together with a little dust. It is believed that the dust particles are pulled quite quickly to the planet's surface, so that they must be formed continually.

The inner two satellites, Cordelia and Ophelia, act as **SHEPHERD SATELLITES** for portions of the rings.

AURORA A region of illumination, often in the form of a wavy curtain, high in the atmosphere of a planet.

CRATER A deep bowl-shaped depression in the surface of a body formed by the high-speed impact of another, smaller body.

GRAVITATIONAL FIELD The region surrounding a body in which that body's gravitational force can be felt.

MAGNETIC FIELD The region of influence of a magnetic body.

MAGNETISM An invisible force that has the property of attracting iron and similar metals.

MASS The amount of matter in an object.

PRESSURE The force per unit area.

RADIATION The transfer of energy in the form of waves (such as light and heat) or particles (such as from radioactive decay of a material).

SATELLITE An object that is in an orbit around another object, usually a planet.

SHEPHERD SATELLITES Larger natural satellites that have an influence on small debris in nearby rings because of their gravity.

SOLAR WIND The flow of tiny charged particles (called plasma) outward from the Sun.

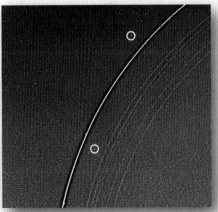

▲ Two shepherd moons *(ringed)* confine one of the rings around Uranus.

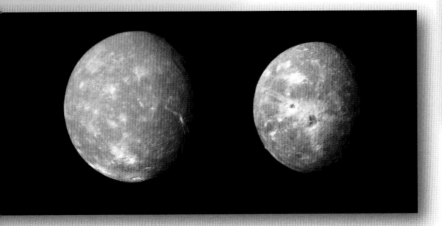

◀ The moons Titania *(far left)* and Oberon *(left)*.

▲ Neptune, whose blue color is caused by methane gas absorbing the red part of the sunlight.

5: NEPTUNE

Neptune is the eighth planet farthest from the Sun and half as far away again from the Sun as Uranus. Neptune is the only gas giant planet that is not visible with the naked eye.

Neptune moves around the Sun in a nearly circular **ORBIT** at a distance of 4.5 billion kilometers. It is about four times the size of the Earth and is roughly the same size as Uranus. Neptune has a **DENSITY** of about 1.6 g/cm³.

As on Uranus, the color of the planet is affected by having an **ATMOSPHERE** that includes methane gas. The gas absorbs strongly in the red part of the spectrum, so that the **REFLECTED** light occurs only in the **COMPLEMENTARY COLOR**, in this case, blue.

Neptune moves once around the Sun every 164.8 Earth years. Each season on Neptune lasts 41 years, although day and night change quickly because each Neptunian day is just 16.1 Earth hours.

Neptune spins on an **AXIS** that is tilted similarly to that of the Earth. In Neptune's case the tilt is 29.6° (Earth's tilt is 23.5°).

At the **EQUATOR** Neptune is 49,528 kilometers across, but it is slightly flattened at the **POLES** due to the **CENTRIFUGAL FORCE** exerted on it as it spins on its axis. Measured across the poles, the diameter is just 48,680 kilometers.

Neptune is so far from the Sun that **SOLAR RADIATION** has little effect. However, Neptune has a small source of internal heat and as a result is somewhat warmer than Uranus. In general, Neptune sends out to space about twice as much heat as it receives from the Sun. This internal heat may help generate the great storms and fast winds seen in the atmosphere of the planet.

The atmosphere

The dominant gas in the atmosphere of Neptune is hydrogen, with helium second in importance. Most of the remaining 2% is methane.

ATMOSPHERE The envelope of gases that surrounds the Earth and other bodies in the universe.

AXIS (pl. **AXES**) The line around which a body spins.

CENTRIFUGAL FORCE A force that acts on an orbiting or spinning body, tending to oppose gravity and move away from the center of rotation.

COMPLEMENTARY COLOR A color that is diametrically opposite another in the range, or circle, of colors in the spectrum; for example, cyan (blue) is the complement of red.

DENSITY A measure of the amount of matter in a space.

EQUATOR The ring drawn around a body midway between the poles.

ORBIT The path followed by one object as it tracks around another.

POLE The geographic pole is the place where a line drawn along the axis of rotation exits from a body's surface.

REFLECT To bounce back any light that falls on a surface.

SOLAR RADIATION The light and heat energy sent into space from the Sun.

▼ Neptune's high-level clouds run in bands above the main cloud mass of the planet.

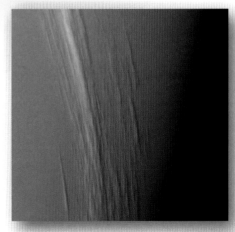

Great Dark Spot

The Scooter

Small Dark Spot

◄ In between the Great Dark Spot and the Small Dark Spot lies the bright region called the Scooter.

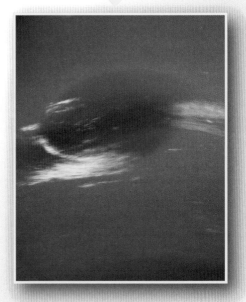

▲ The Great Dark Spot on Neptune, a severe storm with white patches that may represent methane-ice clouds.

Although the edge of Neptune's atmosphere is very cold and just 50 degrees above **ABSOLUTE ZERO** (–223°C), the increase in **PRESSURE** toward the center of the planet causes warming. Near the **CORE** it is probably about 7,000°C. Here the pressure is about five million times Earth's **ATMOSPHERIC PRESSURE**.

In the outer atmosphere there is little movement of air between **LATITUDES**, and winds almost all blow parallel to the equator, some with amazing speeds. At about 20°S winds blow constantly at 700 m/s—the fastest winds known in the solar system. (An Earth tornado may reach 83 m/s, but only briefly.)

The great turbulence in the atmosphere produces storms of upwelling gases that can be seen as dark spots. The Great Dark Spot at 22°S is about the size of the Earth. There is a further Small Dark Spot at about 55°S.

Another important feature of the atmosphere is the bright streaks, nicknamed the Scooter. Each of the dark spots also has a companion bright streak. They may be methane-ice clouds.

Neptune has distinctive cloud layers, with high clouds of methane-ice crystals separated from a bigger and lower cloud bank. It is possible to see the shadow cast by the high cloud on the lower cloud banks.

The core

Neptune is the densest of the giant planets, being almost a third as dense as the Earth. This must mean that it has a larger than usual core, probably made from melted ice and molten rock.

Neptune, like Uranus, has a **MAGNETIC FIELD** that is produced not from its core, as on the Earth or Jupiter or Saturn, but from a region closer to the cloud tops. At the moment there is no clear explanation for why this should be.

The magnetic field traps few charged particles, and so it has none of the spectacular **AURORAS** that are a feature of the larger gas giants.

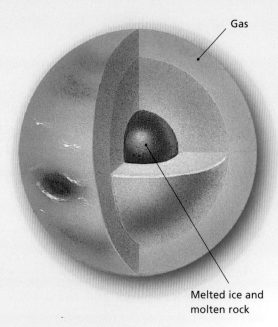

Gas

Melted ice and molten rock

Satellites and rings

From Earth-bound telescopes only two moons can be seen—Triton and Nereid. Voyager's encounter found six others (Naiad, Thalassa, Despina, Galatea, Larissa, and Proteus), all between the surface of Neptune and Triton. Proteus is 400 km across; the others are each about 200 km across.

ABSOLUTE ZERO The coldest possible temperature, defined as 0 K or –273°C.

ATMOSPHERIC PRESSURE The pressure on the gases in the atmosphere caused by gravity pulling them toward the center of a celestial body.

AURORA A region of illumination, often in the form of a wavy curtain, high in the atmosphere of a planet.

CORE The central region of a body.

LATITUDE Angular distance north or south of the equator, measured through 90°.

MAGNETIC FIELD The region of influence of a magnetic body.

PRESSURE The force per unit area.

◀ Neptune's two bright rings have material throughout their orbit and are continuous. The faint inner ring can also be seen.

▶ Neptune's largest moon, Triton.

The small **SATELLITES** appear to be irregular in shape because they are too small for **GRAVITY** to have pulled them into **SPHERES**. They also have many **CRATERS**, suggesting they are of great age. They may represent fragments of material of former moons split up as Triton was captured by Neptune.

Triton

Triton is 2,700 km across and about the same size as the planet Pluto. It is also similar in composition to Pluto, which has prompted the suggestion that it is a former planet from the edge of the solar system that has been captured by Neptune. It is distinctive because it is the only large moon in the solar system to travel against the planet's rotation (it has a **RETROGRADE DIRECTION**).

It has a very **REFLECTIVE** icy surface. The moon seems to be made mainly of water-ice with a rocky core, but the surface is ice made of methane and nitrogen.

The surface seems to erupt **GEYSERS** made of nitrogen gas escaping through the ice to produce plumes that rise up to 8 km above the surface.

The cracked surface is thought to be the result of the capturing of Triton by Neptune. The enormous **GRAVITATIONAL PULL** of the planet may have melted the moon; it then came into **EQUILIBRIUM** with the planet and cooled, the surface cooling first, and finally the core freezing as water-ice, causing expansion, which cracked the surface.

Nereid

Nereid (340 km across) orbits a very long way from the planet in a very **ECCENTRIC** orbit, coming seven times closer to the planet at its nearest point than when it is farthest away. This strange orbit may have been produced as a result of the capturing of Triton, since the approach of that moon would have altered the orbits of everything near Neptune.

CRATER A deep bowl-shaped depression in the surface of a body formed by the high-speed impact of another, smaller body.

ECCENTRIC A noncircular, or oval, orbit.

EQUILIBRIUM A state of balance.

GEYSER A periodic fountain of material. On Earth geysers are of water and steam, but on other planets and moons they are formed from other substances, for example, nitrogen gas on Triton.

GRAVITY/GRAVITATIONAL PULL The force of attraction between bodies. The larger an object, the more its gravitational pull on other objects.

REFLECTIVE To bounce back any light that falls on a surface.

RETROGRADE DIRECTION An orbit the opposite of normal.

SATELLITE An object that is in an orbit around another object, usually a planet.

SPHERE A ball-shaped object.

▶ Neptune as seen from Triton in a superimposed composite view.

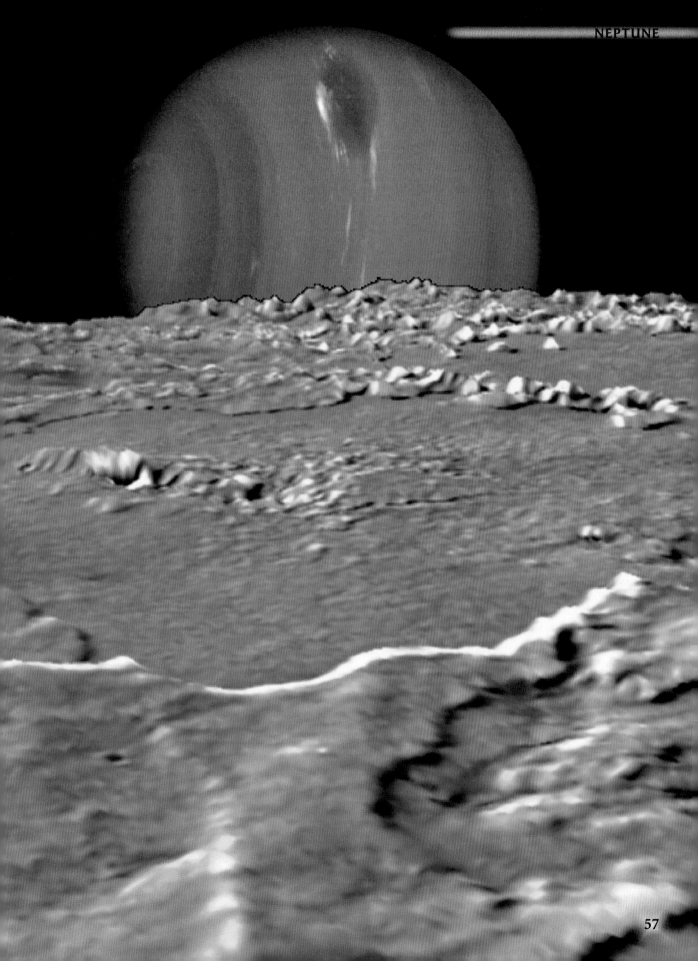

SET GLOSSARY

ABSOLUTE ZERO The coldest possible temperature, defined as 0 K or −273°C.
See also: **K**.

ACCELERATE To gain speed.

AERODYNAMIC A shape offering as little resistance to the air as possible.

AIR RESISTANCE The frictional drag that an object creates as it moves rapidly through the air.

AMINO ACIDS Simple organic molecules that can be building blocks for living things.

ANNULAR Ringlike.
    An annular eclipse occurs when the dark disk of the Moon does not completely obscure the Sun.

ANTENNA (pl. **ANTENNAE**) A device, often in the shape of a rod or wire, used for sending out and receiving radio waves.

ANTICLINE An arching fold of rock layers where the rocks slope down from the crest.

ANTICYCLONE A roughly circular region of the atmosphere that is spiraling outward and downward.

APOGEE The point on an orbit where the orbiting object is at its farthest from the object it is orbiting.

APOLLO The program developed in the United States by NASA to get people to the Moon's surface and back safely.

ARRAY A regular group or arrangement.

ASH Fragments of lava that have cooled and solidified between when they leave a volcano and when they fall to the surface.

ASTEROID Any of the many small objects within the solar system.
    Asteroids are rocky or metallic and are conventionally described as significant bodies with a diameter smaller than 1,000 km. Asteroids mainly occupy a belt between Mars and Jupiter (asteroid belt).

ASTEROID BELT The collection of asteroids that orbit the Sun between the orbits of Mars and Jupiter.

ASTHENOSPHERE The region below the lithosphere, and therefore part of the upper mantle, in which some material may be molten.

ASTRONOMICAL UNIT (**AU**) The average distance from the Earth to the Sun (149,597,870 km).

ASTRONOMY The study of space beyond the Earth and its contents. It includes those phenomena that affect the Earth but that originate in space, such as meteorites and aurora.

ASTROPHYSICS The study of physics in space, what other stars, galaxies, and planets are like, and the physical laws that govern them.

ASYNCHRONOUS Not connected in time or pace.

ATMOSPHERE The envelope of gases that surrounds the Earth and other bodies in the universe.
    The Earth's atmosphere is very different from that of other planets, being, for example, far lower in hydrogen and helium than the gas giants and lower in carbon dioxide than Venus, but richer in oxygen than all the others.

ATMOSPHERIC PRESSURE The pressure on the gases in the atmosphere caused by gravity pulling them toward the center of a celestial body.

ATOM The smallest particle of an element.

ATOMIC MASS UNIT A measure of the mass of an atom or molecule.
    An atomic mass unit equals one-twelfth of the mass of an atom of carbon-12.

ATOMIC WEAPONS Weapons that rely on the violent explosive force achieved when radioactive materials are made to go into an uncontrollable chain reaction.

ATOMIC WEIGHT The ratio of the average mass of a chemical element's atoms to carbon-12.

AURORA A region of illumination, often in the form of a wavy curtain, high in the atmosphere of a planet.
    It is the result of the interaction of the planet's magnetic field with the particles in the solar wind. High-energy electrons from the solar wind race along the planet's magnetic field into the upper atmosphere. The electrons excite atmospheric gases, making them glow.

AXIS (pl. **AXES**) The line around which a body spins.
    The Earth spins around an axis through its north and south geographic poles.

BALLISTIC MISSILE A rocket that is guided up in a high arching path; then the fuel supply is cut, and it is allowed to fall to the ground.

BASIN A large depression in the ground (bigger than a crater).

BIG BANG The theory that the universe as we know it started from a single point (called a singularity) and then exploded outward. It is still expanding today.

BINARY STAR A pair of stars that are gravitationally attracted, and that revolve around one another.

BLACK DWARF A degenerate star that has cooled so that it is now not visible.

BLACK HOLE An object that has a gravitational pull so strong that nothing can escape from it.
    A black hole may have a mass equal to thousands of stars or more.

BLUE GIANT A young, extremely bright and hot star of very large mass that has used up all its hydrogen and is no longer in the main sequence. When a blue giant ages, it becomes a red giant.

BOILING POINT The change of state of a substance in which a liquid rapidly turns into a gas without a change in temperature.

BOOSTER POD A form of housing that stands outside the main body of the launcher.

CALDERA A large pit in the top of a volcano produced when the top of the volcano explodes and collapses in on itself.

CAPSULE A small pressurized space vehicle.

CATALYST A substance that speeds up a chemical reaction but that is itself unchanged.

CELESTIAL Relating to the sky above, the "heavens."

CENTER OF GRAVITY The point at which all of the mass of an object can be balanced.

CENTRIFUGAL FORCE A force that acts on an orbiting or spinning body, tending to oppose gravity and move away from the center of rotation.
    For orbiting objects the centrifugal force acts in the opposite direction from gravity. When satellites orbit the Earth, the centrifugal force balances out the force of gravity.

CENTRIFUGE An instrument for spinning small samples very rapidly.

CHAIN REACTION A sequence of related events with one event triggering the next.

CHASM A deep, narrow trench.

CHROMOSPHERE The shell of gases that makes up part of the atmosphere of a star and lies between the photosphere and the corona.

CIRCUMFERENCE The distance around the edge of a circle or sphere.

COMA The blurred image caused by light bouncing from a collection of dust and ice particles escaping from the nucleus of a comet.

The coma changes the appearance of a comet from a point source of reflective light to a blurry object with a tail.

COMBUSTION CHAMBER A vessel inside an engine or motor where the fuel components mix and are set on fire, that is, they are burned (combusted).

COMET A small object, often described as being like a dirty snowball, that appears to be very bright in the night sky and has a long tail when it approaches the Sun.

Comets are thought to be some of the oldest objects in the solar system.

COMPLEMENTARY COLOR A color that is diametrically opposed in the range, or circle, of colors in the spectrum; for example, cyan (blue) is the complement of red.

COMPOSITE A material made from solid threads in a liquid matrix that is allowed to set.

COMPOUND A substance made from two or more elements that have chemically combined.

Ammonia is an example of a compound made from the elements hydrogen and nitrogen.

CONDENSE/CONDENSATION (1) To make something more concentrated or compact.

(2) The change of state from a gas or vapor to a liquid.

CONDUCTION The transfer of heat between two objects when they touch.

CONSTELLATION One of many commonly recognized patterns of stars in the sky.

CONVECTION/CONVECTION CURRENTS The circulating flow in a fluid (liquid or gas) that occurs when it is heated from below.

Convective flow is caused in a fluid by the tendency for hotter, and therefore less dense, material to rise and for colder, and therefore more dense, material, to sink with gravity. That results in a heat transfer.

CORE The central region of a body.

The core of the Earth is about 3,300 km in radius, compared with the radius of the whole Earth, which is 6,300 km.

CORONA (pl. **CORONAE**) (1) A colored circle seen around a bright object such as a star.

(2) The gases surrounding a star such as the Sun. In the case of the Sun and certain other stars these gases are extremely hot.

(3) A circular to oval pattern of faults, fractures, and ridges with a sagging center as found on Venus. In the case of Venus they are a few hundred kilometers in diameter.

CORONAL MASS EJECTIONS Very large bubbles of plasma escaping into the corona.

CORROSIVE SUBSTANCE Something that chemically eats away something else.

COSMOLOGICAL PRINCIPLE States that the way you see the universe is independent of the place where you are (your location). In effect, it means that the universe is roughly uniform throughout.

COSMONAUT A Russian space person.

COSMOS The universe and everything in it. The word "cosmos" suggests that the universe operates according to orderly principles.

CRATER A deep bowl-shaped depression in the surface of a body formed by the high-speed impact of another, smaller body.

Most craters are formed by the impact of asteroids and meteoroids. Craters have both a depression, or pit, and also an elevated rim formed of the material displaced from the central pit.

CRESCENT The appearance of the Moon when it is between a new Moon and a half Moon.

CRUST The solid outer surface of a rocky body.

The crust of the Earth is mainly just a few tens of kilometers thick, compared to the total radius of 6,300 km for the whole Earth. It forms much of the lithosphere.

CRYSTAL An ordered arrangement of molecules in a compound. Crystals that grow freely develop flat surfaces.

CYCLONE A large storm in which the atmosphere spirals inward and upward.

On Earth cyclones have a very low atmospheric pressure at their center and often contain deep clouds.

DARK MATTER Matter that does not shine or reflect light.

No one has ever found dark matter, but it is thought to exist because the amount of ordinary matter in the universe is not enough to account for many gravitational effects that have been observed.

DENSITY A measure of the amount of matter in a space.

Density is often measured in grams per cubic centimeter. The density of the Earth is 5.5 grams per cubic centimeter.

DEORBIT To move out of an orbital position and begin a reentry path toward the Earth.

DEPRESSION (1) A sunken area or hollow in a surface or landscape.

(2) A region of inward swirling air in the atmosphere associated with cloudy weather and rain.

DIFFRACTION The bending of light as it goes through materials of different density.

DISK A shape or surface that looks round and flat.

DOCK To meet with and attach to another space vehicle.

DOCKING PORT/STATION A place on the side of a spacecraft that contains some form of anchoring mechanism and an airlock.

DOPPLER EFFECT The apparent change in pitch of a fast-moving object as it approaches or leaves an observer.

DOWNLINK A communication to Earth from a spacecraft.

DRAG A force that hinders the movement of something.

DWARF STAR A star that shines with a brightness that is average or below.

EARTH The third planet from the Sun and the one on which we live.

The Earth belongs to the group of rocky planets. It is unique in having an oxygen-rich atmosphere and water, commonly found in its three phases—solid, liquid, and gas.

EARTHQUAKE The shock waves produced by the sudden movement of two pieces of brittle crust.

ECCENTRIC A noncircular, or oval, orbit.

ECLIPSE The time when light is cut off by a body coming between the observer and the source of the illumination (for example, eclipse of the Sun), or when the body the observer is on comes between the source of illumination and another body (for example, eclipse of the Moon).

It happens when three bodies are in a line. This phenomenon is not necessarily called an eclipse. Occultations of stars by the Moon and transits of Venus or Mercury are examples of different expressions used instead of "eclipse."

See also: **TOTAL ECLIPSE.**

ECOLOGY The study of living things in their environment.

ELECTRONS Negatively charged particles that are parts of atoms.

ELEMENT A substance that cannot be decomposed into simpler substances by chemical means.

Elements are the building blocks of compounds. For example, silicon and oxygen are elements. They combine to form the compound silicon dioxide, or quartz.

ELLIPTICAL GALAXY A galaxy that has an oval shape rather like a football, and that has no spiral arms.

EL NIÑO A time when ocean currents in the Pacific Ocean reverse from their normal pattern and disrupt global weather patterns. It occurs once every 4 or 5 years.

EMISSION Something that is sent or let out.

ENCKE GAP A gap between rings around Saturn named for the astronomer Johann Franz Encke (1791–1865).

EPOXY RESIN Adhesives that develop their strength as they react, or "cure," after mixing.

EQUATOR The ring drawn around a body midway between the poles.

EQUILIBRIUM A state of balance.

ESA The European Space Agency. ESA is an organizaton of European countries for cooperation in space research and technology. It operates several installations around Europe and has its headquarters in Paris, France.

ESCARPMENT A sharp-edged ridge.

EVAPORATE/EVAPORATION The change in state from liquid to a gas.

EXOSPHERE The outer part of the atmosphere starting about 500 km from the surface. This layer contains so little air that molecules rarely collide.

EXTRAVEHICULAR ACTIVITY Any task performed by people outside the protected environment of a space vehicle's pressurized compartments. Extravehicular activities (EVA) include repairing equipment in the Space Shuttle bay.

FALSE COLOR The colors used to make the appearance of some property more obvious.
   They are part of the computer generation of an image.

FAULT A place in the crust where rocks have fractured, and then one side has moved relative to the other.
   A fault is caused by excessive pressure on brittle rocks.

FLUORESCENT Emitting the visible light produced by a substance when it is struck by invisible waves, such as ultraviolet waves.

FRACTURE A break in brittle rock.

FREQUENCY The number of complete cycles of (for example, radio) waves received per second.

FRICTION The force that resists two bodies that are in contact.
   For example, the effect of the ocean waters moving as tides slows the Earth's rotation.

FUSION The joining of atomic nuclei to form heavier nuclei.
   This process results in the release of huge amounts of energy.

GALAXY A system of stars and interstellar matter within the universe.
   Galaxies may contain billions of stars.

GALILEAN SATELLITES The four large satellites of Jupiter discovered by astronomer Galileo Galilei in 1610. They are Callisto, Europa, Ganymede, and Io.

GALILEO A U.S. space probe launched in October 1989 and designed for intensive investigation of Jupiter.

GEIGER TUBE A device to detect radioactive materials.

GEOSTATIONARY ORBIT A circular orbit 35,786 km directly above the Earth's equator.
   Communications satellites frequently use this orbit. A satellite in a geostationary orbit will move at the same rate as the Earth's rotation, completing one revolution in 24 hours. That way it remains at the same point over the Earth's equator.

GEOSTATIONARY SATELLITE A man-made satellite in a fixed or geosynchronous orbit around the Earth.

GEOSYNCHRONOUS ORBIT An orbit in which a satellite makes one circuit of the Earth in 24 hours.
   A geosynchronous orbit coincides with the Earth's orbit—it takes the same time to

complete an orbit as it does for the Earth to make one complete rotation. If the orbit is circular and above the equator, then the satellite remains over one particular point of the equator; that is called a geostationary orbit.

GEOSYNCLINE A large downward sag or trench that forms in the Earth's crust as a result of colliding tectonic plates.

GEYSER A periodic fountain of material. On Earth geysers are of water and steam, but on other planets and moons they are formed from other substances, for example, nitrogen gas on Triton.

GIBBOUS When between half and a full disk of a body can be seen lighted by the Sun.

GIMBALS A framework that allows anything inside it to move in a variety of directions.

GLOBAL POSITIONING SYSTEM A network of geostationary satellites that can be used to locate the position of any object on the Earth's surface.

GRANULATION The speckled pattern we see in the Sun's photosphere as a result of convectional overturning of gases.

GRAVITATIONAL FIELD The region surrounding a body in which that body's gravitational force can be felt.
   The gravitational field of the Sun spreads over the entire solar system. The gravitational fields of the planets each exert some influence on the orbits of their neighbors.

GRAVITY/GRAVITATIONAL FORCE/ GRAVITATIONAL PULL The force of attraction between bodies. The larger an object, the more its gravitational pull on other objects.
   The Sun's gravity is the most powerful in the solar system, keeping all of the planets and other materials within the solar system.

GREAT RED SPOT A large, almost permanent feature of the Jovian atmosphere that moves around the planet at about latitude 23°S.

GREENHOUSE EFFECT The increase in atmospheric temperature produced by the presence of carbon dioxide in the air.
   Carbon dioxide has the ability to soak up heat radiated from the surface of a planet and partly prevent its escape. The effect is similar to that produced by a greenhouse.

GROUND STATION A receiving and transmitting station in direct communication with satellites. Such stations are characterized by having large dish-shaped antennae.

GULLY (pl. **GULLIES**) A trench in the land surface formed, on Earth, by running water.

GYROSCOPE A device in which a rapidly spinning wheel is held in a frame in such a way that it can rotate in any direction. The momentum of the wheel means that the gyroscope retains its position even when the frame is tilted.

HEAT SHIELD A protective device on the outside of a space vehicle that absorbs the heat during reentry and protects it from burning up.

HELIOPAUSE The edge of the heliosphere.

HELIOSEISMOLOGY The study of the internal structure of the Sun by modeling the Sun's patterns of internal shock waves.

HELIOSPHERE The entire range of influence of the Sun. It extends to the edge of the solar system.

HUBBLE SPACE TELESCOPE An orbiting telescope (and so a satellite) that was placed above the Earth's atmosphere so that it could take images that were far clearer than anything that could be obtained from the surface of the Earth.

HURRICANE A very violent cyclone that begins close to the equator, and that contains winds of over 117 km/hr.

ICE CAP A small mountainous region that is covered in ice.

INFRARED Radiation with a wavelength that is longer than red light.

INNER PLANETS The rocky planets closest to the Sun. They are Mercury, Venus, Earth, and Mars.

INTERNATIONAL SPACE STATION The international orbiting space laboratory.

INTERPLANETARY DUST The fine dustlike material that lies scattered through space, and that exists between the planets as well as in outer space.

INTERSTELLAR Between the stars.

IONIZED Matter that has been converted into small charged particles called ions.
   An atom that has gained or lost an electron.

IONOSPHERE A part of the Earth's atmosphere in which the number of ions (electrically charged particles) is enough to affect how radio waves move.
   The ionosphere begins about 50 km above the Earth's surface.

IRREGULAR SATELLITES Satellites that orbit in the opposite direction from their parent planet.
   This motion is also called retrograde rotation.

ISOTOPE Atoms that have the same number of protons in their nucleus, but that have different masses; for example, carbon-12 and carbon-14.

JOVIAN PLANETS An alternative group name for the gas giant planets: Jupiter, Saturn, Uranus, and Neptune.

JUPITER The fifth planet from the Sun and two planets farther away from the Sun than the Earth.
   Jupiter is 318 times as massive as the Earth and 1,500 times as big by volume. It is the largest of the gas giants.

K Named for British scientist Lord Kelvin (1824–1907), it is a measurement of absolute temperature. Zero K is called absolute zero and is only approached in deep space: ice melts at 273 K, and water boils at 373 K.

KEELER GAP A gap in the rings of Saturn named for the astronomer James Edward Keeler (1857–1900).

KILOPARSEC A unit of a thousand parsecs. A parsec is the unit used for measuring the largest distances in the universe.

KUIPER BELT A belt of planetesimals (small rocky bodies, one kilometer to hundreds of kilometers across) much closer to the Sun than the Oort cloud.

LANDSLIDE A sudden collapse of material on a steep slope.

LA NIÑA Below normal ocean temperatures in the eastern Pacific Ocean that disrupt global weather patterns.

LATITUDE Angular distance north or south of the equator, measured through 90°.

LAUNCH VEHICLE/LAUNCHER A system of propellant tanks and rocket motors or engines designed to lift a payload into space. It may, or may not, be part of a space vehicle.

LAVA Hot, melted rock from a volcano.

Lava flows onto the surface of a planet and cools and hardens to form new rock. Most of the lava on Earth is made of basalt.

LAVA FLOW A river or sheet of liquid volcanic rock.

LAWS OF MOTION Formulated by Sir Isaac Newton, they describe the forces that act on a moving object.

The first law states that an object will keep moving in a straight line at constant speed unless it is acted on by a force.

The second law states that the force on an object is related to the mass of the object multiplied by its acceleration.

The third law states that an action always has an equal and directly opposite reaction.

LIFT An upthrust on the wing of a plane that occurs when it moves rapidly through the air. It is the main way of suspending an airplane during flight. The engines simply provide the forward thrust.

LIGHT-YEAR The distance traveled by light through space in one Earth year, or 63,240 astronomical units.

The speed of light is the speed that light travels through a vacuum, which is 299,792 km/s.

LIMB The outer edge of a celestial body, including an atmosphere if it has one.

LITHOSPHERE The upper part of the Earth, corresponding generally to the crust and believed to be about 80 km thick.

LOCAL GROUP The Milky Way, the Magellanic Clouds, the Andromeda Galaxy, and over 20 other relatively near galaxies.

LUNAR Anything to do with the Moon.

MAGELLANIC CLOUD Either of two small galaxies that are companions to the Milky Way Galaxy.

MAGMA Hot, melted rock inside the Earth that, when cooled, forms igneous rock.

Magma is associated with volcanic activity.

MAGNETIC FIELD The region of influence of a magnetic body.

The Earth's magnetic field stretches out beyond the atmosphere into space. There it interacts with the solar wind to produce auroras.

MAGNETISM An invisible force that has the property of attracting iron and similar metals.

MAGNETOPAUSE The outer edge of the magnetosphere.

MAGNETOSPHERE A region in the upper atmosphere, or around a planet, where magnetic phenomena such as auroras are found.

MAGNITUDE A measure of the brightness of a star.

The apparent magnitude is the brightness of a celestial object as seen from the Earth. The absolute magnitude is the standardized brightness measured as though all objects were the same distance from the Earth. The brighter the object, the lower its magnitude number. For example, a star of magnitude 4 is 2.5 times as bright as one of magnitude 5. A difference of five magnitudes is the same as a difference in brightness of 100 to 1. The brightest stars have negative numbers. The Sun's apparent magnitude is −26.8. Its absolute magnitude is 4.8.

MAIN SEQUENCE The 90% of stars in the universe that represent the mature phase of stars with small or medium mass.

MANTLE The region of a planet between the core and the crust.

The Earth's mantle is about 2,900 km thick, and its upper surface may be molten in some places.

MARE (pl. **MARIA**) A flat, dark plain created by lava flows. They were once thought to be seas.

MARS The fourth planet from the Sun in our solar system and one planet farther away from the Sun than the Earth.

Mars is a rocky planet almost half the diameter of Earth that is a distinctive rust-red color.

MASCON A region of higher surface density on the Moon.

MASS The amount of matter in an object.

The amount of matter, and so the mass, remains the same, but the effect of gravity gives the mass a weight. The weight depends on the gravitational pull. Thus a ball will have the same mass on the Earth and on the Moon, but it will weigh a sixth as much on the Moon because the force of gravity there is only a sixth as strong.

MATTER Anything that exists in physical form. Everything we can see is made of matter. The building blocks of matter are atoms.

MERCURY The closest planet to the Sun in our solar system and two planets closer to the Sun than Earth.

Mercury is a gray-colored rocky planet less than half the diameter of Earth. It has the most extreme temperature range of any planet in our solar system.

MESOSPHERE One of the upper regions of the atmosphere, beginning at the top of the stratosphere and continuing from 50 km upward until the temperature stops declining.

METEOR A streak of light (shooting star) produced by a meteoroid as it enters the Earth's atmosphere.

The friction with the Earth's atmosphere causes the small body to glow (become incandescent). That is what we see as a streak of light.

METEORITE A meteor that reaches the Earth's surface.

METEOROID A small body moving in the solar system that becomes a meteor if it enters the Earth's atmosphere.

Meteoroids are typically only a few millimeters across and burn up as they go through the atmosphere, but some have crashed to the Earth, making large craters.

MICROMETEORITES Tiny pieces of space dust moving at high speeds.

MICRON A millionth of a meter.

MICROWAVELENGTH Waves at the shortest end of the radio wavelengths.

MICROWAVE RADIATION The background radiation that is found everywhere in space, and whose existence is used to support the Big Bang theory.

MILKY WAY The spiral galaxy in which our star and solar system are situated.

MINERAL A solid crystalline substance.

MINOR PLANET Another term for an asteroid.

M NUMBER In 1781 Charles Messier began a catalogue of the objects he could see in the night sky. He gave each of them a unique number. The first entry was called M1. There is no significance to the number in terms of brightness, size, closeness, or otherwise.

MODULE A section, or part, of a space vehicle.

MOLECULE A group of two or more atoms held together by chemical bonds.

MOLTEN Liquid, suggesting that it has changed from a solid.

MOMENTUM The mass of an object multiplied by its velocity.

MOON The natural satellite that orbits the Earth.

Other planets have large satellites, or moons, but none is relatively as large as our Moon, suggesting that it has a unique origin.

MOON The name generally given to any large natural satellite of a planet.

MOUNTAIN RANGE A long, narrow region of very high land that contains several or many mountains.

NASA The National Aeronautics and Space Administration.

NASA was founded in 1958 for aeronautical and space exploration. It operates several installations around the country and has its headquarters in Washington, D.C.

NEAP TIDE A tide showing the smallest difference between high and low tides.

NEBULA (pl. **NEBULAE**) Clouds of gas and dust that exist in the space between stars.

The word means mist or cloud and is also used as an alternative to galaxy. The gas makes up to 5% of the mass of a galaxy. What a nebula looks like depends on the arrangement of gas and dust within it.

NEPTUNE The eighth planet from the Sun in our solar system and five planets farther away from the Sun than the Earth.

Neptune is a gas planet that is almost four times the diameter of Earth. It is blue.

NEUTRINOS An uncharged fundamental particle that is thought to have no mass.

NEUTRONS Particles inside the core of an atom that are neutral (have no charge).

NEUTRON STAR A very dense star that consists only of tightly packed neutrons. It is the result of the collapse of a massive star.

NOBLE GASES The unreactive gases, such as neon, xenon, and krypton.

NOVA (pl. **NOVAE**) (1) A star that suddenly becomes much brighter, then fades away to its original brightness within a few months. *See also:* **SUPERNOVA**.

(2) A radiating pattern of faults and fractures unique to Venus.

NUCLEAR DEVICES Anything that is powered by a source of radioactivity.

NUCLEUS (pl. **NUCLEI**) The centermost part of something, the core.

OORT CLOUD A region on the edge of the solar system that consists of planetesimals and comets that did not get caught up in planet making.

OPTICAL Relating to the use of light.

ORBIT The path followed by one object as it tracks around another.

The orbits of the planets around the Sun and moons around their planets are oval, or elliptical.

ORGANIC MATERIAL Any matter that contains carbon and is alive.

OUTER PLANETS The gas giant planets Jupiter, Saturn, Uranus, and Neptune plus the rocky planet Pluto.

OXIDIZER The substance in a reaction that removes electrons from and thereby oxidizes (burns) another substance.

In the case of oxygen this results in the other substance combining with the oxygen to form an oxide (also called an oxidizing agent).

OZONE A form of oxygen (O_3) with three atoms in each molecule instead of the more usual two (O_2).

OZONE HOLE The observed lack of the gas ozone in the upper atmosphere.

PARSEC The unit used for measuring the largest distances in the universe.

A parsec is the distance at which an observer in space would see the radius of the orbit as making one second of arc. This gives a distance of about 3.26 light-years.

See also: **KILOPARSEC**.

PAYLOAD The spacecraft that is carried into space by a launcher.

PENUMBRA (1) A region that is in semidarkness during an eclipse.

(2) The part of a sunspot surrounding the umbra.

PERCOLATE To flow by gravity between particles, for example, of soil.

PERIGEE The point on an orbit where the orbiting object is as close as it ever comes to the object it is orbiting.

PHARMACEUTICAL Relating to medicinal drugs.

PHASE The differing appearance of a body that is closer to the Sun, and that is illuminated by it.

PHOTOCHEMICAL SMOG A hazy atmosphere, often brown, resulting from the reaction of nitrogen gases with sunlight.

PHOTOMOSAIC A composite picture made up of several other pictures that individually only cover a small area.

PHOTON A particle (quantum) of electromagnetic radiation.

PHOTOSPHERE A shell of the Sun that we regard as its visible surface.

PHOTOSYNTHESIS The process that plants use to combine the substances in the environment, such as carbon dioxide, minerals, and water, with oxygen and energy-rich organic compounds by using the energy of sunlight.

PIONEER A name for a series of unmanned U.S. spacecraft.

Pioneer 1 was launched into lunar orbit on October 11, 1958. The others all went into deep space.

PLAIN A flat or gently rolling part of a landscape.

Plains are confined to lowlands. If a flat surface exists in an upland, it is called a plateau.

PLANE A flat surface.

PLANET Any of the large bodies that orbit the Sun.

The planets are (outward from the Sun): Mercury, Venus, Earth, Mars, Jupiter, Saturn, Uranus, Neptune, and Pluto. The rocky planets all have densities greater than 3 grams per cubic centimeter; the gaseous ones less than 2 grams per cubic centimeter.

PLANETARY NEBULA A compact ring or oval nebula that is made of material thrown out of a hot star.

The term "planetary nebula" is a misnomer; dying stars create these cocoons when they lose outer layers of gas. The process has nothing to do with planet formation, which is predicted to happen early in a star's life.

The term originates from a time when people, looking through weak telescopes, thought that the nebulae resembled planets within the solar system, when in fact they were expanding shells of glowing gas in far-off galaxies.

PLANETESIMAL Small rocky bodies one kilometer to hundreds of kilometers across.

The word especially relates to materials that exist in the early stages of the formation of a star and its planets from the dust of a nebula, which will eventually group together to form planets. Some are rock, others a mixture of rock and ice.

PLANKTON Microscopic creatures that float in water.

PLASMA A collection of charged particles that behaves something like a gas. It can conduct an electric charge and be affected by magnetic fields.

PLASTIC The ability of certain solid substances to be molded or deformed to a new shape under pressure without cracking.

PLATE A very large unbroken part of the crust of a planet. Also called tectonic plate.

On Earth the tectonic plates are dragged across the surface by convection currents in the underlying mantle.

PLATEAU An upland plain or tableland.

PLUTO The ninth planet from the Sun and six planets farther from the Sun than the Earth.

Pluto is one of the rocky planets, but it is very different from the others, perhaps being a mixture of rock and ice. It is about two-thirds the size of our Moon.

POLE The geographic pole is the place where a line drawn along the axis of rotation exits from a body's surface.

Magnetic poles do not always correspond with geographic poles.

POLYMER A compound that is made up of long chains formed by combining molecules called monomers as repeating units. ("Poly" means many, "mer" means part.)

PRESSURE The force per unit area.

PROBE An unmanned spacecraft designed to explore our solar system and beyond.

Voyager, Cassini, and Magellan are examples of probes.

PROJECTILE An object propelled through the air or space by an external force or an on-board engine.

PROMINENCE A cloud of burning ionized gas that rises through the Sun's chromosphere into the corona. It can take the form of a sheet or a loop.

PROPELLANT A gas, liquid, or solid that can be expelled rapidly from the end of an object in order to give it motion.

Liquefied gases and solids are used as rocket propellants.

PROPULSION SYSTEM The motors or rockets and their tanks designed to give a launcher or space vehicle the thrust it needs.

PROTEIN Molecules in living things that are vital for building tissues.

PROTONS Positively charged particles from the core of an atom.

PROTOSTAR A cloud of gas and dust that begins to swirl around; the resulting gravity gives birth to a star.

PULSAR A neutron star that is spinning around, releasing electromagnetic radiation, including radio waves.

QUANTUM THEORY A concept of how energy can be divided into tiny pieces called quanta, which is the key to how the smallest particles work and how they build together to make the universe around us.

QUASAR A rare starlike object of enormous brightness that gives out radio waves, which are thought to be released as material is sucked toward a black hole.

RADAR Short for radio detecting and ranging. A system of bouncing radio waves from objects in order to map their surfaces and find out how far away they are.

Radar is useful in conditions where visible light cannot be used.

RADIATION/RADIATE The transfer of energy in the form of waves (such as light and heat) or particles (such as from radioactive decay of a material).

RADIOACTIVE/RADIOACTIVITY The property of some materials that emit radiation or energetic particles from the nucleus of their atoms.

RADIOACTIVE DECAY The change that takes place inside radioactive materials and causes them to give out progressively less radiation over time.

RADIO GALAXY A galaxy that gives out radio waves of enormous power.

RADIO INTERFERENCE Reduction in the radio communication effectiveness of the ionosphere caused by sunspots and other increases in the solar wind.

RADIO TELESCOPE A telescope that is designed to detect radio waves rather than light waves.

RADIO WAVES A form of electromagnetic radiation, like light and heat. Radio waves have a longer wavelength than light waves.

RADIUS (pl. **RADII**) The distance from the center to the outside of a circle or sphere.

RAY A line across the surface of a planet or moon made by material from a crater being flung across the surface.

REACTION An opposition to a force.

REACTIVE The ability of a chemical substance to combine readily with other substances. Oxygen is an example of a reactive substance.

RED GIANT A cool, large, bright star at least 25 times the diameter of our Sun.

REFLECT/REFLECTION/REFLECTIVE To bounce back any light that falls on a surface.

REGULAR SATELLITES Satellites that orbit in the same direction as their parent planet. This motion is also called synchronous rotation.

RESOLVING POWER The ability of an optical telescope to form an image of a distant object.

RETROGRADE DIRECTION An orbit the opposite of normal—that is, a planet that spins so the Sun rises in the west and sinks in the east.

RETROROCKET A rocket that fires against the direction of travel in order to slow down a space vehicle.

RIDGE A narrow crest of an upland area.

RIFT A trench made by the sinking of a part of the crust between parallel faults.

RIFT VALLEY A long trench in the surface of a planet produced by the collapse of the crust in a narrow zone.

ROCKET Any kind of device that uses the principle of jet propulsion, that is, the rapid release of gases designed to propel an object rapidly.

The word is also applied loosely to fireworks and spacecraft launch vehicles.

ROCKET ENGINE A propulsion system that burns liquid fuel such as liquid hydrogen.

ROCKET MOTOR A propulsion system that burns solid fuel such as hydrazine.

ROCKETRY Experimentation with rockets.

ROTATION Spinning around an axis.

SAND DUNE An aerodynamically shaped hump of sand.

SAROS CYCLE The interval of 18 years $11^1/_3$ days needed for the Earth, Sun, and Moon to come back into the same relative positions. It controls the pattern of eclipses.

SATELLITE (1) An object that is in an orbit around another object, usually a planet.

The Moon is a satellite of the Earth.
See also: **IRREGULAR SATELLITE, MOON, GALILEAN SATELLITE, REGULAR SATELLITE, SHEPHERD SATELLITE.**

(2) A man-made object that orbits the Earth. Usually used as a term for an unmanned spacecraft whose job is to acquire or transfer data to and from the ground.

SATURN The sixth planet from the Sun and three planets farther away from the Sun than the Earth.

It is the least-dense planet in the solar system, having 95 times the mass of the Earth, but 766 times the volume. It is one of the gas giant planets.

SCARP The steep slope of a sharp-crested ridge.

SEASONS The characteristic cycle of events in the heating of the Earth that causes related changes in weather patterns.

SEDIMENT Any particles of material that settle out, usually in layers, from a moving fluid such as air or water.

SEDIMENTARY Rocks deposited in layers.

SEISMIC Shaking, relating to earthquakes.

SENSOR A device used to detect something. Your eyes, ears, and nose are all sensors. Satellites use sensors that mainly detect changes in radio and other waves, including sunlight.

SHEPHERD SATELLITES Larger natural satellites that have an influence on small debris in nearby rings because of their gravity.

SHIELD VOLCANO A volcanic cone that is broad and gently sloping.

SIDEREAL MONTH The average time that the Moon takes to return to the same position against the background of stars.

SILT Particles with a range of 2 microns to 60 microns across.

SLINGSHOT TRAJECTORY A path chosen to use the attractive force of gravity to increase the speed of a spacecraft.

The craft is flown toward the planet or star, and it speeds up under the gravitational force. At the correct moment the path is taken to send the spacecraft into orbit and, when pointing in the right direction, to turn it from orbit, with its increased velocity, toward the final destination.

SOLAR Anything to do with the Sun.

SOLAR CELL A photoelectric device that converts the energy from the Sun (solar radiation) into electrical energy.

SOLAR FLARE Any sudden explosion from the surface of the Sun that sends ultraviolet radiation into the chromosphere. It also sends out some particles that reach Earth and disrupt radio communications.

SOLAR PANELS Large flat surfaces covered with thousands of small photoelectric devices that convert solar radiation into electricity.

SOLAR RADIATION The light and heat energy sent into space from the Sun.

Visible light and heat are just two of the many forms of energy sent by the Sun to the Earth.

SOLAR SYSTEM The Sun and the bodies orbiting around it.

The solar system contains nine major planets, at least 60 moons (large natural satellites), and a vast number of asteroids and comets, together with the gases within the system.

SOLAR WIND The flow of tiny charged particles (called plasma) outward from the Sun.

The solar wind stretches out across the solar system.

SONIC BOOM The noise created when an object moves faster than the speed of sound.

SPACE Everything beyond the Earth's atmosphere.

The word "space" is used rather generally. It can be divided up into inner space—the solar system, and outer space—everything beyond the solar system, for example, interstellar space.

SPACECRAFT Anything capable of moving beyond the Earth's atmosphere. Spacecraft can be manned or unmanned. Unmanned spacecraft are often referred to as space probes if they are exploring new areas.

SPACE RACE The period from the 1950s to the 1970s when the United States and the Soviet Union competed to be first in achievements in space.

SPACE SHUTTLE NASA's reusable space vehicle that is launched like a rocket but returns like a glider.

SPACE STATION A large man-made satellite used as a base for operations in space.

SPEED OF LIGHT *See:* **LIGHT-YEAR.**

SPHERE A ball-shaped object.

SPICULES Jets of relatively cool gas that move upward through the chromosphere into the corona.

SPIRAL GALAXY A galaxy that has a core of stars at the center of long curved arms made of even more stars arranged in a spiral shape.

SPRING TIDE A tide showing the greatest difference between high and low tides.

STAR A large ball of gases that radiates light. The star nearest the Earth is the Sun.

There are enormous numbers of stars in the universe, but few can be seen with the naked eye. Stars may occur singly, as our Sun, or in groups, of which pairs are most common.

STAR CLUSTER A group of gravitationally connected stars.

STELLAR WIND The flow of tiny charged particles (called plasma) outward from a star.

In our solar system the stellar wind is the same as the solar wind.

STRATOSPHERE The region immediately above the troposphere where the temperature increases with height, and the air is always stable.

It acts like an invisible lid, keeping the clouds in the troposphere.

SUBDUCTION ZONES Long, relatively thin, but very deep regions of the crust where one plate moves down and under, or subducts, another. They are the source of mountain ranges.

SUN The star that the planets of the solar system revolve around.

The Sun is 150 million km from the Earth and provides energy (in the form of light and heat) to our planet. Its density of 1.4 grams per cubic centimeter is similar to that of a gas giant planet.

SUNSPOT A spiral of gas found on the Sun that is moving slowly upward, and that is cooler than the surrounding gas and so looks darker.

SUPERNOVA A violently exploding star that becomes millions or even billions of times brighter than when it was younger and stable.

See also: **NOVA.**

SYNCHRONOUS Taking place at the same time.

SYNCHRONOUS ORBIT An orbit in which a satellite (such as a moon) moves around a planet in the same time that it takes for the planet to make one rotation on its axis.

SYNCHRONOUS ROTATION When two bodies make a complete rotation on their axes in the same time.

As a result, each body always has the same side facing the other. The Moon and Venus are in synchronous rotation with the Earth.

SYNODIC MONTH The complete cycle of phases of the Moon as seen from Earth. It is 29.531 solar days (29 days, 12 hours, 44 minutes, 3 seconds).

SYNODIC PERIOD The time needed for an object within the solar system, such as a planet, to return to the same place relative to the Sun as seen from the Earth.

TANGENT A direction at right angles to a line radiating from a circle or sphere.

If you make a wheel spin, for example, by repeatedly giving it a glancing blow with your hand, the glancing blow is moving along a tangent.

TELECOMMUNICATIONS Sending messages by means of telemetry, using signals made into waves such as radio waves.

THEORY OF RELATIVITY A theory based on how physical laws change when an observer is moving. Its most famous equation says that at the speed of light, energy is related to mass and the speed of light.

THERMOSPHERE A region of the upper atmosphere above the mesosphere.

It absorbs ultraviolet radiation and is where the ionosphere has most effect.

THRUST A very strong and continued pressure.

THRUSTER A term for a small rocket engine.

TIDE Any kind of regular, or cyclic, change that occurs due to the effect of the gravity of one body on another.

We are used to the ocean waters of the Earth being affected by the gravitational pull of the Moon, but tides also cause a small alteration of the shape of a body. This is important in determining the shape of many moons and may even be a source of heating in some.

See also: **NEAP TIDE** and **SPRING TIDE.**

TOPOGRAPHY The shape of the land surface in terms of height.

TOTAL ECLIPSE When one body (such as the Moon or Earth) completely obscures the light source from another body (such as the Earth or Moon).

A total eclipse of the Sun occurs when it is completely blocked out by the Moon.

A total eclipse of the Moon occurs when it passes into the Earth's shadow to such a degree that light from the Sun is completely blocked out.

TRAJECTORY The curved path followed by a projectile.

See also: **SLINGSHOT TRAJECTORY.**

TRANSPONDER Wireless receiver and transmitter.

TROPOSPHERE The lowest region of the atmosphere, where all of the Earth's clouds form.

TRUSS Tubing arrayed in the form of triangles and designed to make a strong frame.

ULTRAVIOLET A form of radiation that is just beyond the violet end of the visible spectrum and so is called "ultra" (more than) violet. At

the other end of the visible spectrum is "infra" (less than) red.

UMBRA (1) A region that is in complete darkness during an eclipse.

(2) The darkest region in the center of a sunspot.

UNIVERSE The entirety of everything there is; the cosmos.

Many space scientists prefer to use the term "cosmos," referring to the entirety of energy and matter.

UNSTABLE In atmospheric terms the potential churning of the air in the atmosphere as a result of air being heated from below. There is a chance of the warmed, less-dense air rising through the overlying colder, more-dense air.

UPLINK A communication from Earth to a spacecraft.

URANUS The seventh planet from the Sun and four planets farther from the Sun than the Earth.

Its diameter is four times that of the Earth. It is one of the gas giant planets.

VACUUM A space that is entirely empty. A vacuum lacks any matter.

VALLEY A natural long depression in the landscape.

VELOCITY A more precise word to describe how something is moving, because movement has both a magnitude (speed) and a direction.

VENT The tube or fissure that allows volcanic materials to reach the surface of a planet.

VENUS The second planet from the Sun and our closest neighbor.

It appears as an evening and morning "star" in the sky. Venus is very similar to the Earth in size and mass.

VOLCANO A mound or mountain that is formed from ash or lava.

VOYAGER A pair of U.S. space probes designed to provide detailed information about the outer regions of the solar system.

Voyager 1 was launched on September 5, 1977. Voyager 2 was launched on August 20, 1977, but traveled more slowly than Voyager 1. Both Voyagers are expected to remain operational until 2020, by which time they will be well outside the solar system.

WATER CYCLE The continuous cycling of water, as vapor, liquid, and solid, between the oceans, the atmosphere, and the land.

WATER VAPOR The gaseous form of water. Also sometimes referred to as moisture.

WEATHERING The breaking down of a rock, perhaps by water, ice, or repeated heating and cooling.

WHITE DWARF Any star originally of low mass that has reached the end of its life.

X-RAY An invisible form of radiation that has extremely short wavelengths just beyond the ultraviolet.

X-rays can go through many materials that light will not.

SET INDEX

A

absolute zero **4**: 46, **5**: 54, **7**: 57
accretion (buildup) disk **1**: 36, 37, 39
active galactic nucleus **1**: 36, 37. *See also* black holes
Adrastea (Jupiter moon) **5**: 34, 35
aerodynamic design, rockets **6**: 7, 16, 22, **7**: 17
Agena (rocket) **6**: 41
air resistance **6**: 6, 7, 22
Albor Tholus (Mars volcano) **4**: 41
Aldrin, Jr., E. "Buzz" **3**: 44, **6**: 50
Alpha Regio (Venus) **4**: 25
aluminum, Earth **3**: 39
Amalthea (Jupiter moon) **5**: 34, 35
amino acids **4**: 54
ammonia:
    gas giants **5**: 6
    rocky planets **5**: 6
    Saturn **5**: 39
    Uranus **5**: 49
    See also ammonia-ice
ammonia-ice:
    comets **4**: 54
    Jupiter **5**: 14, 15
    Neptune **5**: 6
    Saturn **5**: 39, 40
    Uranus **5**: 6
Andromeda Galaxy (M31) **1**: 11, 12, 40–41, 50
antenna (pl. antennae) **6**: 31, 40, 52, 53, 54, 55, **7**: 6, 7, 26, 33, 38, **8**: 8, 49, 51, 57
anticyclones **5**: 10, 14, **8**: 20
apogee **3**: 8, 14
Apollo (Moon mission) **3**: 2, 4–5, 16–17, 44–45, 47, 48–49, 51, 52, 54, **6**: 2, 6, 10, 20, 42–51, **7**: 4, 17, 33, 34, 35, 44. *See also* Saturn (launcher)

Apollo applications program. *See* Skylab (space station)
Aqua (satellite) **8**: 14–15, 42
argon:
    Earth **3**: 22
    Moon **3**: 44
Ariane (launcher) **6**: 20, **8**: 10
Ariel (Uranus moon) **5**: 50, 51
Aristarchus (Greek thinker) **1**: 6
Aristarchus (Moon crater) **3**: 50
Armstrong, Neil **6**: 49, 50
Arsia Mons (Mars volcano) **4**: 41
Ascraeus Mons (Mars volcano) **4**: 41
ash:
    Earth **3**: 32, 39, 41
    Mercury **4**: 19
    See also lava
asteroid belt **2**: 47, **4**: 48, 49–50, 57, **6**: 54. *See also* Kirkwood gaps
asteroids **1**: 5, **2**: 4, 46, 51, **4**: 5, 48–52
    collisions with **2**: 51, 53, **4**: 9, 10, 11, 50, 51, 52, **5**: 21
    comet origin **4**: 48
    composition **2**: 51, **4**: 10, 51
    description **4**: 10, 48
    formation **2**: 54, **4**: 11, 50, 51
    irregular **4**: 11, 51
    Mars' moons **4**: 42
    mass **2**: 49, **4**: 51
    meteorite from **4**: 6
    numbers of **4**: 49
    orbits **2**: 46, 47, 51, **4**: 10, 48, 49, 50–51, 52, **6**: 57
    rotation **4**: 51
    See also asteroid belt; Astraea; Ceres; Eros; Gaspra; Hygiea; Ida; Juno; Pallas; Vesta
asthenosphere:
    Earth **3**: 31, 34
    Moon **3**: 55
Astraea (asteroid) **4**: 48
astronauts:
    Apollo (Moon mission) **3**: 44, 45, 46, **6**: 43, 44–45, 46, 47, 49, 50, 51
    endurance **7**: 46
    exercise **7**: 33, 35, 38, 39, 54
    Gemini **6**: 38–39, 41
    gravity, effect of **6**: 41, **7**: 9, 10, 22, **8**: 30
    living space **7**: 23, 33, 34, 39, 41, 45, 50, 53–54
    showering **7**: 34, 35
    space, effect of **7**: 53, 54, 55
    weight **3**: 42
    weightlessness **6**: 16, **7**: 42
    See also cosmonauts; extravehicular activity; manned spaceflight
astronomical unit (AU), definition **1**: 10
astronomy **1**: 42, **7**: 56–57, **8**: 15, 54
astrophysics laboratory (Mir) **7**: 38, 41
asynchronous orbit **8**: 13
Atlantis (Space Shuttle) **7**: 2, 23, 36–37, 40–41
Atlas (launcher) **6**: 19, 35
Atlas (Saturn moon) **5**: 40, 41, 45
atomic mass units **2**: 9
atomic structure **7**: 54
atomic weapons **6**: 18. *See also* ballistic missiles
atomic weight **1**: 14
atoms **1**: 6, 14, 16, 17, 23, 26, 30, 54, 56, **2**: 8, 9, 12, 16, 22, 40, 45, 56, 57, **3**: 24, **4**: 54, **5**: 24, **7**: 57. *See also* atomic structure
Aurora Australis **3**: 21

Aurora Borealis **3**: 21
auroras:
    Earth **2**: 15, 38, 44–45, **3**: 19, 20–21, 24
    Ganymede **5**: 32
    Jupiter **5**: 16
    Uranus **5**: 50

B

ballistic missiles (ICBMs) **6**: 16, 17, 18–19
Beta Regio (Venus) **4**: 25
Betelgeuse (star) **2**: 13, 14
Big Bang **1**: 54, 55, 56, **7**: 55, **8**: 57
binary stars **1**: 18, 26, 30, 36
black dwarf stars **1**: 21, 29, **2**: 11
black holes **1**: 2, 5, 33, 35–39, 45, **8**: 56, 57
blue giants **1**: 14, 17, 22–23, 36, 51, **2**: 12, **8**: 54
Bok globules **1**: 14
booster pods (Russian launchers) **6**: 18, 19
boosters. *See under* Space Shuttle
Borrelly (comet) **4**: 52
bow shock **2**: 40, 41, 42
Butterfly Nebula **1**: 26, **2**: 10

C

calcium:
    stars **1**: 30
    Sun **2**: 16
    universe **1**: 14, 16
Callisto (Galilean satellite) **2**: 55, **5**: 8, 18–19, 30, 33–34
Caloris Basin (Mercury) **4**: 17, 18
Calypso (Saturn moon) **5**: 40, 41
Canada **2**: 45, **3**: 35, **7**: 45, 49, **8**: 21, 25, 42
Candor Chasm (Mars) **4**: 39
carbon:
    Callisto **5**: 34
    comets **4**: 54
    Earth **3**: 5, 16
    interplanetary dust **4**: 10
    Space Shuttle tiles **7**: 28
    stars **1**: 19, 26, 29, **2**: 11
    Sun **2**: 11, 17
    Titan **5**: 42
carbon dioxide:
    comets **4**: 53
    Earth **3**: 22, 27, 30, **4**: 36
    Mars **4**: 34. *See also* carbon dioxide ice
    Venus **4**: 23, 24, 25
carbon dioxide ice (dry ice), Mars **4**: 31, 32, 33, 34
carbon monoxide, comets **4**: 53
Cassini, Giovanni **3**: 9
Cassini division **5**: 44, 46
Cassini-Huygens (probe) **5**: 37, **6**: 21, 56, 57
Cat's Eye Nebula **1**: 26–27
Centaur (launcher) **6**: 21, 56
center of gravity:
    binary stars **1**: 18
    Earth and Moon **3**: 8, 54
centrifugal forces:
    Earth **3**: 10, 18, **4**: 22
    Moon **3**: 10
    Neptune **5**: 53
    satellites **8**: 10
    Saturn **5**: 39
    science fiction **7**: 42
    spacecraft **7**: 10, 42
    Uranus **5**: 49
    Venus **4**: 22
ceramic tiles, heat protection on Space Shuttle **7**: 27–28
Ceres (asteroid) **4**: 10, 48, 51
Cernan, Gene **6**: 51
Challenger (Space Shuttle) **7**: 23, 26–27
Chamberlin, Chrowder **2**: 53
Charon (Pluto moon) **4**: 44, 46–47, 57

Chasma Borealis (Mars) **4**: 32
chromosphere **2**: 18, 22, 32, 33, 35
circumference:
    Earth **3**: 18
    Mars **4**: 41
COBE (satellite) **8**: 57
Columbia (Space Shuttle) **7**: 17, 23, 26
coma (comet) **2**: 51, **4**: 52, 53, 55
combustion chamber. *See* engines
Comet Borrelly **4**: 52
comets **1**: 5, **2**: 4, 46, 51–52, **4**: 5, 6, 8, 10, 47, 48, 53–55
    atmosphere **4**: 53
    collisions with **2**: 52, 53, **5**: 21
    coma **2**: 51, **4**: 52, 53, 55
    Comet Borrelly **4**: 52
    composition **2**: 51, **4**: 8, 10, 53, 54, **5**: 34
    gravitational field **4**: 54
    Halley's Comet **4**: 54, 55
    lifespan **4**: 55
    mass **2**: 14, 49
    nucleus **2**: 51, **4**: 52, 53, 54
    orbits **2**: 51, 52, **4**: 52, 53, 54, 57
    radiation **4**: 53
    Shoemaker-Levy 9 **4**: 53
    tails **2**: 38, 51, **4**: 53, 54
    word origin **4**: 53
    See also Kuiper belt; Oort cloud; *and under* ammonia-ice; carbon; carbon dioxide; carbon monoxide; dust; hydrogen; ice, water; methane; methane-ice; nitrogen; oxygen; plasma; rock; sulfur; water vapor
complementary color **5**: 49, 53
condensation:
    dust formation **1**: 26
    planet and moon formation **2**: 49, 54, **4**: 8, **5**: 4, 6, 17, 18
    water vapor **3**: 23, 29, **4**: 8
conduction **3**: 23, 55
constellations **1**: 8–9
    Andromeda **1**: 9, 23, 40, 41
    Aquila **1**: 9, 30, **6**: 54
    Circinus **1**: 8, 37
    Crux (Southern Cross) **1**: 8
    Draco **1**: 8, 9, 26–27, 47
    Gemini **1**: 8, 28
    Hydra **1**: 8, 35
    Lyra **1**: 9, 12
    Monoceros **1**: 8, 26
    Orion **1**: 8, 9, 13, 17
    Pegasus **1**: 9, 12
    Sagittarius **1**: 9, 11, 17, 18, 25
    Serpens **1**: 8, 16
    Taurus **1**: 9, 13, **6**: 54
    Ursa Major (Great Bear) **1**: 8
    Virgo **1**: 8, 39
    Vulpecula **1**: 9, 13
continental drift **3**: 36–37
convection/convection currents:
    Earth **3**: 23, 29, 32–33, 36
    Ganymede **5**: 32
    Jupiter **5**: 12
    Mars **4**: 36
    Sun **2**: 22, 23, 26, 28
    Venus **4**: 29
convective zone **2**: 18–19, 22, 23
Cooper, Jr., Gordon **6**: 35, 37
Copernicus **1**: 6, **2**: 48
Cordelia (Uranus moon) **5**: 51
corona (pl. coronae) (star) **2**: 19, 22, 35–37, 38, 41, 53, **3**: 15
corona (pl. coronae) (Venus) **4**: 27
coronal loops **2**: 35, 36–37. *See also* prominences
coronal mass ejections **2**: 4–5, 22–23, 35, 44
Cosmic Background Explorer (COBE) **8**: 57
Cosmological Principle **1**: 42, 49
cosmonauts **6**: 31, 32–33, 35, 39, **7**: 30, 32, 39, 41, 46, **8**: 30